ASP.... C-Level Business Intelligence™

Praise for Books, Briefs, Journals & Guides:

"Tremendous insights...a must read..." - James Quinn, Litigation Chair, Weil, Gotshal & Manges

"Great information for business executives and employers of any size." - Judy Langevin, Employment Chair, Gray, Plant, Mooty, Mooty & Bennett

"A rare peek behind the curtains and into the minds of the industry's best." - Brandon Baum, Partner, Cooley Godward

"Intensely personal, practical advice from seasoned dealmakers." - Mary Ann Jorgenson, Coordinator of Business Practice Area, Squire, Sanders & Dempsey

"What C-Level executives read to keep their edge and make pivotal business decisions. Timeless classics for indispensable knowledge." - Richard Costello, Manager-Corporate Marketing Communication, General Electric (NYSE: GE)

"True insight from the doers in the industry, as opposed to the critics on the sideline." - Steve Hanson, CEO, On Semiconductor (NASDAQ: ONNN)

"Unlike any other business books, Inside the Minds captures the essence, the deep-down thinking processes, of people who make things happen." - Martin Cooper, CEO, Arraycomm

"The only useful way to get so many good minds speaking on a complex topic." - Scott Bradner, Senior Technical Consultant, Harvard University

INSIDE THE MINDS

**Empowering Professionals of All Levels
With C-Level Business Intelligence**
www.InsideTheMinds.com

The critically acclaimed *Inside the Minds* series provides readers of all levels with proven business intelligence from C-Level executives (CEO, CFO, CTO, CMO, Partner) from the world's most respected companies. Each chapter is comparable to a white paper or essay and is a future-oriented look at where an industry/profession/topic is heading and the most important issues for future success. Each author has been carefully chosen through an exhaustive selection process by the *Inside the Minds* editorial board to write a chapter for this book. *Inside the Minds* was conceived in order to give readers actual insights into the leading minds of business executives worldwide. Because so few books or other publications are actually written by executives in industry, *Inside the Minds* presents an unprecedented look at various industries and professions never before available.

For information on bulk orders, sponsorship opportunities or any other questions, please email store@aspatore.com.

For information on licensing the content in this book, or any content published by Aspatore, please email jonp@aspatore.com.

To nominate yourself, another individual, or a group of executives for an upcoming Inside the Minds book, or to suggest a specific topic for an Inside the Minds book, please email jason@aspatore.com.

ASPATORE
C-Level Business Intelligence™

Publisher of Books, Business Intelligence Publications & Services

www.Aspatore.com

Aspatore is the world's largest and most exclusive publisher of C-Level executives (CEO, CFO, CTO, CMO, Partner) from the world's most respected companies. Aspatore annually publishes C-Level executives from over half the Global 500, top 250 professional services firms, law firms (MPs/Chairs), and other leading companies of all sizes in books, briefs, reports, articles and other publications. By focusing on publishing only C-Level executives, Aspatore provides professionals of all levels with proven business intelligence from industry insiders, rather than relying on the knowledge of unknown authors and analysts. Aspatore publishes an innovative line of business intelligence resources including Inside the Minds, Bigwig Briefs, ExecRecs, Business Travel Bible, Brainstormers, The C-Level Test, and Aspatore Business Journals, in addition to other best selling business books, briefs and essays. Aspatore also provides an array of business services including The C-Level Library, PIA Reports, SmartPacks, and The C-Level Review, as well as outsourced business library and researching capabilities. Aspatore focuses on traditional print publishing and providing business intelligence services, while our portfolio companies, Corporate Publishing Group (B2B writing & editing), Aspatore Speaker's Network, and Aspatore Stores focus on developing areas within the business and publishing worlds.

INSIDE THE MINDS:
Leading Lawyers
The Art & Science of Being a Successful Lawyer

ASPATORE
C-Level Business Intelligence™

**If you are interested in forming a business partnership
with Aspatore or licensing the content in this book (for
publications, web sites, educational materials),
purchasing bulk copies for your team/company with
your company logo, or for sponsorship, promotions or
advertising opportunities, please email
store@aspatore.com or call toll free 1-866-Aspatore.**

Published by Aspatore, Inc.

For corrections, company/title updates, comments or any other inquiries please email
info@aspatore.com.

First Printing, November 2002
10 9 8 7 6 5 4 3 2

ISBN 1-58762-150-9

Inside the Minds Managing Editor, Carolyn Murphy, Edited by Jo Alice Hughes,
Proofread by Ginger Conlon, Cover design by Kara Yates & Ian Mazie

Material in this book is for educational purposes only. This book is sold with the
understanding that neither any of the authors or the publisher is engaged in rendering
medical, legal, accounting, investment, or any other professional service. For legal
advice, please consult your personal lawyer.

This book is printed on acid free paper.

A special thanks to all the individuals that made this book possible.

Special thanks to: Kirsten Catanzano, Melissa Conradi, Molly Logan, Justin Hallberg

The views expressed by the individuals in this book (or the individuals on the cover) do
not necessarily reflect the views shared by the companies they are employed by (or the
companies mentioned in this book). The companies referenced may not be the same
company that the individual works for since the publishing of this book.

Inside the Minds:
Leading Lawyers
The Art & Science of Being a Successful Lawyer

Contents

ENTERING THE LEGAL PROFESSION

WILLIAM H. BREWSTER

Kilpatrick Stockton LLP

Managing Partner

Find a Mentor and Stay Busy

The legal profession used to be less specialized than it is now, just as being a doctor today can mean so many more things than it did even 20 years ago. Attorneys used to be general business advisors, as opposed to people you call when there is a problem. Given today's environment, there are certain areas of the law I encourage people to be involved in, while there are other aspects I view as likely to be less interesting in the long run. From my point of view, the closer you are to the business issues and the closer you can get to working with the client and helping them achieve their business goals, the better the professional opportunity.

The number-one way to learn legal skills is by working with more experienced lawyers. If you have the right mentor and the right team of lawyers working in your area, you can learn a tremendous amount. Certainly, people can go out on their own and create a practice, learn an area of the law, and become expert in it. But those people are really extraordinary, and they have chosen a very difficult approach. The best way to learn is to work with people who have been in the trenches – people who have learned what works from their own mistakes and can help you avoid making the same errors.

In the pursuit of new skills, you receive much of your best experience when you are extremely busy, particularly when you are in a trial or in the midst of a deal. When you work with a team to produce a brief, you will find that much of the best thinking and action on it occurs in the heat of battle, rather than when deadlines are less pressing and collaboration is not present. Sitting down with one or more people at a table and hashing out the argument will produce the best results.

The importance of going to a top law school depends on what you want to do. There is no question that going to a better school will afford you more opportunities, and you will have more options when you graduate. However, if you have done well at any law school, you will have excellent options available to you. The top students at any law school are roughly equivalent; it is really a question of how deep in the classes the opportunities will be available. At a better law school, those opportunities might be available further down into the class. It also depends on what you are interested in. If you want to be litigator, going to a local school is probably best.

Success in Litigation or Negotiation

For any lawyer, the ability to listen is essential to success. Listening is the first step: If you do not hear the information, you cannot do anything with it. The next step is the ability to apply real-world, practical knowledge to the situations you are handling. For example, I deal primarily with trademarks and brands, so understanding the marketplace, how products are sold, and how consumers receive information from advertising or messages in a supermarket provides critical background to the advice I convey to clients. It is extremely important to have a very strong, practical business side to your experience. Later, your ability to identify key facts and issues, and then effectively convey that information to a client, the opposition, a judge, a jury, or whoever your audience is, will benefit from that practical knowledge.

I have done a lot of litigation, but I have also done a great deal of counseling and conflict resolution and negotiation of agreements. If success in litigation means being able to prevail in a trial, you need two things: a client who has a stomach for litigation, which requires a large amount of time and money, and stubborn lawyers on the other side. In most cases, you do not get a chance to win at trial, because the matter ought to be settled before that stage. Clearly, if a case does go to trial, having good facts is critical.

In terms of negotiation, I try to put myself in the other side's shoes. After I have thought through our position and our perspective, I will make that leap and imagine what the other side is seeing and hearing. Whether you are negotiating an agreement or trying to settle a dispute, the biggest problem is not understanding the other side's concerns. I do the best job I can to figure out what factors are influencing them. If I have a hard time figuring out their motivations, then I will do my best to figure that out over the course of a negotiation.

If you can put yourself in another person's shoes – whether you are dealing with a witness, a client, or the opposition – you tend to be able to defuse arguments. If you can say to the other side, "I understand what you are saying; now let me get you to put yourself in my client's shoes," you will make progress. You don't have to say to them, "You are wrong. I am right." You can just demonstrate to them the difference of opinion or reasoning that needs to be brought to bear.

Being persuasive is about credibility and honesty. If you are in court trying to persuade a judge, you hope to have a reservoir of goodwill based on being forthright and honest with the judge. If she asks you a question, you answer it not only as an advocate, but as an officer of the court. You explain there are two sides of the argument, and while you argue in favor of one side, you must be honest. The same principle holds for the opposition: If you mislead them during a stage of a negotiation or while in litigation, then your ability to be persuasive later – in settlement discussions or otherwise – will be destroyed. Obviously, your clients need to trust you, and your ability to persuade them to follow one course as opposed to another depends on their trusting you.

Acting in the Client's Interest

The art of being a lawyer principally involves client relations. Just as people in business or real estate refer to the phrase "Location, Location, Location," lawyers would be well advised to use the phrase "Client, Client, Client." Dealing with a client properly means listening, a skill that can be learned and certainly improved upon with time. Another aspect of client relations is being able to care about and empathize with your client, something that cannot be faked; all good lawyers appreciate that fact.

You frequently have to help your client see the other side's position. The client may be reluctant to resolve a matter or settle it, preferring to act on principle. Tell them to put themselves in the other side's shoes, recognizing the principles of the other side, and they will acknowledge the best solution is to resolve the matter amicably.

Lawyers and clients alike need to recognize that efforts to resolve matters are not a sign of weakness. Early in a matter, even when I think our side is 100 percent right, I will make sure to make it clear to the people involved that we should, at various stages, talk about how to resolve the matter. When we do so, it's not because we are afraid that we are going to lose a motion or the case, but instead because we think it is in everybody's best interest. Invariably, when you sit down with two businesspeople and attempt to explain to them why they should resolve a matter, the lawyers become their common enemies. If you can say to them, "If we go forward in this case, we lawyers are going to make a lot of money; so, in theory, it is in our interest to let this matter proceed. But you will spend a lot of money and put the matter in the hands of someone who doesn't understand your business – a judge or a jury. You should save yourself the time and aggravation of litigation and eliminate the uncertainty by acting to try to resolve the issue."

I try to make it clear from the beginning of a case that I will push settlement at every stage in the process. That way, if we feel we want to explore settlement later in the case, it won't be perceived as though we fear a particular outcome. You need to constantly reinforce the notion that there are alternatives to litigation that work. This defuses the reluctance to avoid discussing settlement and takes away the fear surrounding the initial offer of settlement, which frequently keeps people from resolving cases.

Successful lawyers recognize they need to be constantly thinking about their client's interests, and that the client's interests, from a business standpoint, will almost always be to resolve a matter before having it decided by a third party. Your line in the sand may be closer or further away, depending on how strong your position is, but nobody should believe going to trial is the best option for their client, absent remarkable circumstances. Those circumstances do occasionally present themselves, but most of the time it is a matter of having the client's interests in mind. That's a litmus test of a good lawyer: The ability to resolve a matter when the time is right, short of having a hearing or having to file a motion or go to trial.

The Challenge of Time Management

The most challenging aspect of practicing law is the lack of time. When I started in law, you had a certain amount of time to respond to a letter. That schedule accelerated if someone thought the letter was actually important enough to send it overnight or by fax. Now, with more advanced modes of communication, everything is done much more quickly, and the expectations are that you will respond

17

instantaneously. Because the practice of law is so dependent on other people's schedules – what the client needs, what the opposition is demanding, what the court has set as a schedule – we do not have the flexibility to decide to do one thing today and another thing tomorrow. We cannot exclude those external influences, so we have to be able to juggle our time commitments effectively.

The challenge of time management is difficult, and your ability to set aside time for your family and personal life is often one of the struggles you face. I try to balance and rebalance my personal and professional lives constantly. The best way to accomplish this balance is by setting that time aside – for example, making appointments to attend a child's game, or to talk to his or her teacher, or to do the things you know you need to do. If you schedule those activities in, the rest of the job can work around them.

In a way, lawyers have a luxury that many business people do not have: Very little about our job requires that we punch a clock at a particular time. If I know I want to be somewhere in the afternoon, then I can come in early and get my work done. I don't have to be sitting in my office at a particular time in the afternoon, and this gives me a chance to go to a school play or a meeting. We have a degree of flexibility in what we do; we are not working for a plant or a factory, or in any typical nine-to-five job. If you have something personal planned, and a client or associate wants to meet with you then, 99.9 percent of the time they will understand your personal obligations. You have to be zealous about it – time can be taken away from you. Fight for it; if you say you have something else scheduled but can have the meeting any other time, people will almost always work with you.

In addition to the regular demands of client work, you also need to read a great deal to stay on top of your practice area. For me, that means reading a lot of material reflecting broad business trends, in addition to legal material. I read a lot about branding, consumers, trends, and product innovations – these issues are discussed in a broad range of publications. I spend a tremendous amount of time reading newspapers and non-legal magazines. Most of these contain general business or consumer-oriented material, which helps me get and keep a sense of what is happening in the rest of the world.

Leading a Firm and Building a Team

A partner ought to be a leader. There are certainly leaders who are not partners; and I think we have associates who are great leaders. At the same time, there are some partners who are still developing their leadership skills. In a law firm environment, to become both a leader and a partner, you need to have good legal skills. Much of what we look for in potential partners is the respect that comes from having topnotch skills. After that, your ability to become a partner depends on your ability to communicate. Many incredibly bright people do not communicate particularly well, and that is the major obstacle to their professional advancement. There is no substitute for good and effective communication skills.

A good attorney also needs common sense. This does not always come as readily as it should to some lawyers. To become a partner and a leader in a law firm, you need to respect others, demonstrate confidence in others, build a team, and do the fairly basic things people know they need to do but sometimes forget when they walk into the office.

The toughest part of leading a firm is dealing with what you perceive as minor administrative issues. The frustration that comes from dealing with the minor, day-to-day questions is the real challenge because it detracts from your ability to spend time on the larger, policy-oriented or client-related issues. The more time you spend on those internal issues, the less time you have to spend on the important external ones. If we are worried about an internal, structural, or administrative issue about a practice group, then we are not spending time worrying about the client or the client's needs. Undoubtedly, the toughest part is getting past those minor issues, which can consume all of your time if you let them.

One of the biggest challenges in the legal profession is staying organized in the face of many competing demands. One of the real keys to that is having the people you work with understand what needs your attention and what does not. For example, the job of any good young lawyer is to make the life of the people they are working with easier. If they can handle problems and deal with situations, they will succeed. Staying organized is one of those challenges I do not have to worry about; my assistant ensures that we meet deadlines. I do not have to worry about what will happen next because the people I am working with will put it in front of me or handle it well themselves. Organization, for me, depends on other people.

I doubt that building a team in a legal practice is very different from doing so in any other context. I do not believe the efficiency of most of the people I work with is based on particular economic incentives or specific rewards. They do it because they enjoy it; there is *esprit de corps,* camaraderie, and an understanding of people's roles in helping the team and helping a client. When people are doing a good job, they know it, and others know it. If things are not going so well, then we spend time working it out with them. Developing and sustaining a team is a constant process.

Ethics and Service

There is clearly an ethical code among lawyers. Some areas of law, such as the trademark bar, are still relatively small compared to the universe of lawyers. This small world means you can generally be sure you will run across another lawyer more than once. If I have a case today against somebody, I will have a case in a couple of years against perhaps the same individual, or someone else from their firm. Certainly, the consequence of that is that you have to live with the decisions you make and your conduct. That's why it is very important to maintain your credibility with anyone in any situation; its loss will affect you later on. I think most lawyers recognize that; certainly, the good ones do.

Honesty and integrity are essential in gaining the respect of the people you practice with, your opponents, third parties – judges, juries, mediators – and anybody else. If you haven't been forthright and honest, you are in a very difficult position. Making certain you treat people well and are honest with them, treating them in the way you would expect or want them to deal with you, is probably the most important golden rule.

Lawyers have an important obligation, based on their position, to make sure they do what they can to help people meet the general legal needs of the population. In other words, they must provide *pro bono* legal support and advice, participate in organizations designed to ensure the justice system operates effectively, and make sure the things they do that no one else can do – being a member of the bar and a lawyer – are done well.

More broadly, because of their experience, background, education, and skills, lawyers are in a better position than most to help efforts to improve society at large. These improvements come through involvement in government and charitable organizations, serving on boards, and developing initiatives designed to improve the quality of life not only for themselves but for others, as well. Lawyers in particular ought to take advantage of that ability, and most of them do; they are active in their communities and disproportionately active in government and charitable groups. Organizations that depend on a high level of outside support generally include more lawyers than other professionals.

The Future of Law: Technology and Globalization

The Internet has been the most significant technological development for the legal profession. The Internet's growth and expansion have posed a tremendous number of challenges for the practice of law. Though the law had general rules in place to govern issues with the Internet, the pace with which new issues arose, such as domain name, priority rights, and trademark and domain name issues, was very rapid and significant.

It is important to consistently update your clients with new legal developments, but unfortunately, time does not often permit you to engage in individual conversations with each of your clients. One approach is to take advantage of e-mail and Web pages and forward information you have received from one particular source to a broad number of clients. This provides your clients with valuable information in a format they can choose to read or review the information when it's convenient for them.

Most legal issues will become increasingly global in the next five years. There has been a tremendous amount of globalization of intellectual property issues. That has developed in the last few years and will accelerate in the next five years. Globalization affects other areas of the law as well, including the legal profession itself. More firms are becoming multinational and international, a trend that has really followed the clients. Just as businesses have consolidated and become international, the law, while a little behind, is starting to catch up. Over the next five years, that will accelerate dramatically.

William H. Brewster is the managing partner at Kilpatrick Stockton and former practice group leader of the Intellectual Property practice group. Mr. Brewster's practice includes client counseling and litigation in the fields of trademark, copyright, false advertising, unfair competition, trade secrets, and restrictive covenants. He is an adjunct professor at the Emory University School of Law, where he teaches trademark law, and also has served on the adjunct faculty at the University of Virginia School of Law.

Mr. Brewster is active in International Trademark Association (INTA) activities, including past service on the Publications and U.S. Legislation Committees and current service on the Brand Names Education Foundation Committee, and coordinating the firm's role as the Southeast Region host for BNEF's Saul Lefkowitz Moot Court competition. Mr. Brewster is the Chair of the Trademark Litigation Committee of the American Intellectual Property Law Association (AIPLA), a member of the Legal Advisory Committee of the Association of Collegiate Licensing Administrators (ACLA), a member of the National Collegiate Licensing Association (NCLA), and a member of the State Bar of Georgia's Antitrust, Intellectual Property and Sports & Entertainment Sections.

USING VISION TO SHAPE LAWYERS AND LAW FIRMS

MARY B. CRANSTON

Pillsbury Winthrop LLP

Chair

"A Great Lawyer": Start with a Vision

The more I have been involved in the law, the more I have come to view it as a service that allows our society and culture to work. The law is a set of ground rules that keep the economy going and our criminal justice systems working, and the lawyers, who are experts in these rules, are there to assist the society and culture in getting business done.

From my experience, one of the critical steps to becoming a great lawyer is developing a strong vision for yourself. This vision is so individualized that each lawyer needs to decide what being a "great lawyer" means to her or him. Once lawyers have established their vision, they go a step further: They do what they need to do to get there. This inner drive is the most important quality of a great lawyer. You need to decide what you want to do and where you want to go in your career. Picture yourself having achieved that vision. Keep this picture of yourself in mind with every decision you make, even the minute-to-minute decisions that seem minor or insignificant at the time. If you are clear about where you want to end up, you will get there.

Great lawyers also recognize that people contribute in different ways; they work to figure out what their own strongest attribute is and how to capitalize on that attribute. For example, you may have a great mind for putting details of the law together, or you may be particularly skilled in how you tell the story to the jury. I believe each person is brilliant in several ways, which is why it is important to set your own goals. If you discover what you do better than anyone else in the world, you have found your niche. Then you can go for it to achieve your vision.

Certainly, becoming a good lawyer involves some aspects of basic talent. There is a technical side to being a lawyer and it takes a lot of discipline and study to achieve depth and understanding of the specific rules – how they interrelate, where the gray areas in the rules are, and what the policy implications are behind the decisions made. Then there is the art, which is putting all of that together in a way that can be understood by your clients and by the non-clients you are trying to persuade. The art has to do with a person's ability to read situations and people, think creatively, and demonstrate advocacy skills. Again, developing these skills comes down to the commitment of the individual. A great lawyer has worked to hone all of these qualities, mastering both the science *and* the art.

Let me expand somewhat on the art of negotiating. Negotiations come down to understanding where everybody is coming from. That often requires you to drop your own blinders and try to put yourself in the shoes of the other person. Whether it is a contentious negotiation to try to settle a lawsuit or a more creative action where you try to come up with a new deal structure, the first and most important thing is to understand where the other person is coming from. It is also very important to always be honest and straightforward – although that does not mean you put everything on the table at the beginning. Further, it is also important to keep your own emotions out of the negotiation process. The discussion should be kept on an even keel emotionally. A lawyer's most important quality for winning a case is an ability to articulate the client's perspective in a way that is both legally correct and emotionally true. That requires a good set of advocacy skills, optimism, and an ability to clarify where you are going in the proceedings, whether before a court or a jury.

In addition to establishing your vision and developing your skills, you also must adhere to some absolute requirements you cannot violate as a lawyer. One requirement is that you uphold ethical standards. You also have to be straightforward, courageous, tell your clients when there is a problem, and confront conflicts. Those qualities are absolutely essential. I believe very strongly in this, so I will say it again. Every lawyer, no matter what, needs to be a complete straightshooter.

I do not believe there is one correct way to be in terms of personality, or that only certain kinds of people make effective lawyers. I believe you can be a brilliant lawyer and be very kind. Whatever your particular package of skills, intelligence, and intuition, you can be a good lawyer if you really want to be. Although you may initially need to take some time to figure out what kind of law is appropriate for you, you will find your area. With regard to other lawyers around me, I respect high-quality legal thinking and the ability to take a set of facts and laws and make a difference by developing some new, creative win-win plan in litigation or business. I respect and require integrity. I also respect compassion and kindness.

I believe these qualities will be just as important in the future as they are today. And lawyers who develop and realize a strong vision and who consistently meet high ethical standards will always become our great lawyers.

Learning, Growing, and Defining Success

Law school is just the beginning of learning the legal skills you need to become a successful lawyer. Finding the best way to develop your skills depends on what you want to do. If you want to be a litigator, you would be well served to watch what goes on in a courtroom. Choosing a law firm that is committed to providing its lawyers with excellent in-house training and mentoring is also helpful. Years ago it would have been possible for young lawyers in big firms to get their trial skills by doing "slip and falls" for major clients, but those kinds of cases are not handled in big firms anymore. Today and in the future, young lawyers have a better chance to develop skills through an in-house university that allows lawyers to study trial skills, get practice, and place themselves in simulated situations.

On the business side, much of the training still comes from working with experienced lawyers, although attending as much backup classroom training as possible is also a good idea. If you want to become a sophisticated lawyer, you will probably need to go to a big firm right out of law school because they have the resources to train you and probably the clients and cases that are cutting edge. I expect this to be the case in the future, too.

I am frequently asked by new lawyers from just about every practice area how they can develop the timeless skill of persuasion. In courses taught in law school and elsewhere, you can learn about the skill and observe people who are very good at persuasion. But developing the skill takes time. Once you enter the work environment, you will see people who are effective, and you can watch what they do and try to imitate it. Borrow from these examples, and tailor what they do to your style. These skills do develop with time; I was not a very good public speaker when I started, but I was committed to learning from other people. Eventually, I grew into my public speaking style and now feel comfortable speaking in front of a variety of audiences.

I am also asked about how to develop intuition. The key here is to watch people who are gifted in terms of reading people well. You can watch how they handle situations, and then practice the skills you've observed.

No matter what kind of law or size of firm interests you, you will ultimately be responsible for your growth. So, to figure out what training would best help you achieve your goals, you will need to do your homework; never assume someone is looking out for you. Very importantly, you need to commit deeply to lifelong learning and work to strengthen your skill sets throughout your career. This will help you and your clients.

In building my own skills, I have always tried to be realistic about my skill set and what I need it to be to get to the next level. I also try to be clear about where I am aiming. For example, when I became a partner, I set a goal for myself that I wanted to control a certain amount of business, because that is one of the ways you gain influence in a law firm. It is also a symbol of your effectiveness in the external market as a trial lawyer. I set some goals for myself in terms of the size of the business I wanted to control and the type of clients I wanted to work with, and then I did an inventory of what I had done until then, what I had not done, and what I needed to do. I began very consciously following a step-by-step plan to try to get the experience I needed to get the recognition I needed in the external marketplace. It took me about five years, but by staying tightly focused on where I was going, and by keeping specific goals and methods in mind, I was able to achieve it. Many people get lost by not being as focused as they should be on where they are trying to go. Being very clear about where you are going makes it a lot easier to know what the important things are and how to prioritize your time each day.

The definition of success is probably different for each individual. Most lawyers would agree on some things that success includes: bringing a high-value job to your client, getting the results the client wants and needs, working with the client to make sure the client understands what the law can and cannot do, and ending up with a situation where the client is satisfied and justice is done.

It is important, though, that each individual set a personal vision. For me, that definition has changed over the years. Fifteen years ago I would have defined my personal success as becoming a recognized trial lawyer who had the opportunity to represent companies through very significant litigation that had a potentially high impact on the companies, and being the lead lawyer in that situation. Once that was achieved, I had to set a new definition of success. At the moment I am working on one that has to do with how I can serve and be of most use. I resist the notion that there is some absolute standard or one thing that is success because it is much more individual than that.

There is a distinction between personal success and success for the client – which most good lawyers work to define with the client. It is very relationship-specific.

To help grow our lawyers' personal and professional success, we have "full commitment plans" that people complete annually. The plan is basically a statement about what the lawyer aspires to accomplish that year. It is reviewed by the management of the firm at the beginning of the year, so we have a pretty good dialogue with every partner about what we expect and what we would like them to do, and we also hear from them about what they would like to do. We have the firm organized to meet client needs, so everyone works with a team to assess and meet our clients' needs. It is a very powerful device that allows lawyers in a non-threatening way to understand the clients' needs and sell themselves to the firm and to understand our business. Rather than telling our partners they need to go out and sell, which is a threatening notion to many lawyers, we give them a lot of support, and we have a very sophisticated marketing staff and knowledge management structure to help the lawyers understand what the clients are doing and where they are headed. This is a powerful set of tools to help our lawyers be successful. Finally, we have a very team-based culture. We do expect everybody to be their brother's and sister's keeper, and to help each other out. It is a great way to make sure lawyers succeed.

Using Vision in a Law Firm

Establishing a vision and setting goals are absolutely the most important things a person ever does. When I set personal goals for myself, I get away by myself for a day every now and then to think about the direction of my life and where it needs to go next. I use my intuition to help me see the future.

I apply similar methods with the firm in conjunction with my management team; about every three years we do a major strategic exercise where we focus on the external market, how it has changed, what our goals are, and where we should be going. My principal strategy is to work with my partners to establish a clear vision.

Over the years I have become quite a student of vision. Vision has intrigued man for centuries; there is a tremendous amount of literature on vision, some from the business press, some from the sports press, and some in the spiritual tradition. Vision is actually a tool that can be used to effect change, especially in an environment where change is taking place all the time. You need a basic change strategy, and for me that strategy is vision.

I work with a number of partners in our firm who are gifted with strategic thinking, and we tend to come up with a first draft of where we are going. Then we take it out to the partners, the staff, and the associate attorneys, and we talk about our vision and modify where we are going based on their input. We then adopt the vision, which becomes a very clear set of specifics about the direction we are moving, or a plan. We keep our vision in mind and measure ourselves against it; we talk about it all the time and constantly evaluate our actions so that we continue to move toward that vision. We hold ourselves accountable. That is the basic strategy that has worked. It is more of a process than a procedure.

What has led us over the past few years and will continue to lead us in the next few years is a vision of an increasingly globalized platform focused on certain legal specialties and arenas. These specialties are not only significant in today's marketplace but are likely to be very important services that our clients will need as they themselves globalize.

Our firm's current strategic plan has only four goals, which are very clear and very straightforward, and everybody knows them and works on them every day. I often use a rowing analogy. There is so much about rowing that is very similar to what we are doing here: There is a very clear goal, which is to get the gold medal, and everybody has to get in the boat and very precisely pull their oars together in maximum effort. In my strategic planning, the whole concept that we put together is to create something as simple as that gold medal for everybody to keep in mind, and then every day, wherever you are in the firm, you pull your oar together to move the whole organization toward the goal. I have found that one of the reasons I am so committed to vision is that I have used it over and over in my own life to create things. Sometimes things that seemed almost impossible when I started – things I knew I wanted to achieve but had no idea how to do – happened when I set the vision and stayed with it.

Demonstrating Leadership and Facing Challenges

My role as the head of the firm comes with some significant challenges because I am the ultimate decision-maker for a very large number of people, not only the lawyers but the staff as well. It is also a 125-year old organization, so I have a great sense of being the current caretaker of something that is bigger than I am. That is a major responsibility.

As a leader, if you have a clear vision of where you are going, you really cannot have an off day. You have to always be moving toward that goal, articulating that goal, having confidence in that goal, and seeing it happen. It is a job that requires some psychological maturity and strength.

Leadership requires a willingness to take on the job of being a leader. Saying, "I will be a leader" means making a choice to take a risk. You put yourself out there as the leader and become the face of the firm. You have to have courage. You need to have a natural facility for big-picture thinking and the ability to stay on the creative side, as opposed to seeing all the problems. You cannot be unaware of issues and problems, though, so you have to be a person who fundamentally enjoys the creative process of fixing all the problems. It also requires an ability to articulate in an upbeat way where the organization is going, and to hold that vision in the light for everyone. You need to have a sense of the needs and aspirations of the key professionals of the firm and the ability to command their confidence. You have to be someone they come to when they have an issue so that you always know what is going on. You have to be willing to hear and actually go out and affirmatively seek helpful feedback that will make you a better leader. One of the problems of being a leader is that people tend to tell you what they think you want to hear, and that is not what you need to hear. You need to hear what you are not seeing; you need to know what you are not doing perfectly and what you are not doing as well as you might. So it takes the courage to constantly ask for that kind of feedback and to set up procedures where you'll get it.

One of the least enjoyable parts of my role as a leader is that I sometimes have to make hard choices. For example, if a piece of our business is not robust and is an area of law that is not growing, we sometimes have to shut down some parts of our business. I have to talk to the people involved, and that can prove personally challenging. But I have grown to the point where I do realize, for everybody, when one door closes, another door opens. I am reassured in my decision-making for this firm, and I aim to help the affected people see that a new situation may be better for them in the long run; I encourage them to find a better situation, where they can serve and be successful. So I have realized that if everyone is honest about what works and what doesn't, and if we all try to have a law firm where everybody's piece makes a contribution to the greater whole, it is ultimately a better allocation of everybody's time, including the time of those who may need to leave us.

Being willing to take risks is absolutely essential. Never taking a risk is one of the riskiest strategies you can follow because that makes you a passive floater at the mercy of the environment. Risk is really about making choices, and in an ever-changing environment the one thing that does not change is that change is there. In the presence of change, you constantly have to make choices, and that is taking risks. If you do that enough and have confidence in yourself, you will soon find you have much more control over your own destiny. Making choices and taking risks then become, in the long run, less scary and more empowering.

In deciding what risks to take, you certainly use your mind to analyze what is going on around you, but fundamentally, you need to use your intuition. Intuition is a more powerful computer than your mind; I think intuition takes more into account. It tells you whether choice A or choice B is more life enhancing, and which one has more energy in it for you. Then you go that way.

In addition to the challenges of leadership, there are also many challenges in the profession in general right now. One is the way the business model has been working in sophisticated firms, where the productivity of the firm is being measured more and more by billable hours and the personal time commitment people make. It is a terribly significant challenge for many because we have reached the end of what can be done with that model; I do not think people can work any harder. In fact, we have many burned-out professionals, in part because of the very difficult, demanding hours we work. The profession has some real issues in terms of where it all connects. We need to think of different ways of measuring ourselves and pricing ourselves so that we can figure out a way to balance life a little better. We are losing a generation of women, for example, because of the stresses of balancing a family with a demanding job.

The progress that has been made in the last 25 years for women is breathtaking on one level, but it is also not enough. Some significant issues still have to do with our cultural expectations about who our leaders are. When I became chair of Pillsbury Winthrop in 1999, I was stunned to learn I was the first woman ever elected to run a major top-100 law firm in the United States. Even since then, there has been only one other, and I do not think she is head anymore. If you look at the partnership ranks, the numbers are way below what the demographics would lead you to expect, given how long women have been coming out of law school. I think we need to continue to pay attention to this. I would really like this not to be an issue by the time my daughter is my age.

Balancing the professional and personal aspects of my life has been difficult at times. I certainly remember when my children were very small and during their junior high era, it was difficult because I always felt I did not have quite enough time for anything. It is like everything else in life – you need to prioritize and determine what is essential and make sure you get that done. My children always knew that if they really needed me, I would drop anything, but they were also very competent kids and respectful enough not to cry wolf. So it worked out well. They are both great kids. My husband is a professional and has always had an understanding about my life and my ambitions. We just try to keep communication channels as clear as possible and make sure everybody knows what is happening; I got everybody cell phones very early. It has been doable, and for me it has been the right mix because I am a very high-energy person and enjoy having a lot of responsibility.

I am a very big advocate of part-time programs. A number of law firms, including my own, manage these programs very well. We have exceptional partners who are part-time for a number of years when their children are small or when they have elderly parents. Some firms still think it does not work, so of course it does not for them. It goes back to what your vision is and what is possible. I believe it is possible, and in fact it does work well. My managing partner was part-time when she became a partner, and she was part-time when she became my managing partner of the firm, so it is very workable. This allows firms to offer women a lifetime career in a law firm that works.

Another significant challenge is that the basic business model that most of the large firms in the U.S. have followed for 50 years is changing rapidly. It has changed a great deal in the last 10 years and will probably change even more, as it is driven by the underlying technological revolution and the global implications of that revolution. The traditional marketplace for many of these firms is changing. Their clients are globalizing or merging out of existence or being acquired, and the firms have to change their business plans to go along with that. It is more change than any of these firms have seen over the last 100 years.

So it requires a strategic and creative skill set that was not called upon before. Many people see these changes as very stressful. It is stressful, but it is also greatly invigorating if you can realize that change is not necessarily a bad thing.

Advice from the Ages

My grandfather, the CEO of a Fortune 500 company, told me this: "A business that is not recreating itself every day is dying." That was pretty insightful for someone who was leading companies in the 1960s and 1970s, and I think it is absolutely true.

One quote that has had a strong influence on me is from Winston Churchill: "You make a living by what you get. You make a life by what you give." That to me is a very powerful statement. Henry Ford said, "Obstacles are the scary things you see when you take your eyes off the goal." I really grew with that – there are a lot of things out there that feel very risky and scary, but if you are focusing on where you are going and making choices to move yourself toward your goal, much of that fear and many of the obstacles fall away; they never rise to anything you need to worry about.

If you want to be successful as a lawyer, you'll need to keep a few golden rules in mind. First, be absolutely straight with everybody in all aspects of your life. Second, remember that the clients are the most important thing, and your job is not just to accept as a passive vehicle your clients' demands, but to put your heart and soul into figuring out the very best thing for them. Third and finally, be compassionate to everyone.

Mary B. Cranston is chair of Pillsbury Winthrop LLP. Her extensive experience includes complex class action litigation, antitrust counseling and litigation, regulated industries counseling and litigation, and securities litigation. Before being elected chair of the firm, Ms. Cranston served as chair of the firm's Litigation Department and on the firm's committees on Compensation, Professional Recruitment, Finance, Legal Education, Partnership Selection, Communications, and Marketing and Client Service.

Honors and awards Ms. Cranston has won include the Anti-Defamation League Distinguished Jurisprudence Award in May 2000; being named to the National Law Journal's list of The 100 Most Influential Lawyers in America in June 2000; being named to the California Daily Journal list of The 100 Most Influential Lawyers in California 1999, 2000, and 2001; being named to the San Francisco Business Times List of the 50 Most Influential Business Women in the Bay Area, 1999 - 2002; the Stanford Associates Award for distinguished service to Stanford University, 1999; and the Summit Award for Women Explorers from the Learning for Life Program, December 2000.

Ms. Cranston has served as an officer of the ABA Antitrust Section and is a past chair of the Antitrust and Trade Regulation Section of the California State Bar. She is a frequent speaker at substantive antitrust programs and an editor of Antitrust Law Developments. A contributing author to Sample Jury Instructions in Civil Antitrust Cases, The Antitrust Evidence Handbook, and Unfair Competition, she is also the author of a treatise on California antitrust law in State Antitrust Practice and Statutes.

A trustee of Stanford University since 2000, Ms. Cranston earned her BA at Stanford, her MA at the University of California at Los Angeles, and her JD at Stanford Law School, where she was a member of the Law Review.

THE ART OF BECOMING A GREAT LAWYER: COMPETENCE, COMMITMENT, AND THE ABILITY TO TRULY LISTEN TO CLIENTS

WALTER DRIVER, JR.

King & Spalding

Chairman

Competence First

Particularly in the early days of a lawyer's career, when the learning curve is very steep, there are enormous long term benefits in simply investing a great deal of time and effort in the development of the very highest legal and professional skills. The demographics of American lawyers show it is not essential to attend the top law schools to become successful. The benefit of attending a top law school is the stimulation of being with other very bright people from whom you can learn. In any law school you can get the same base technical expertise you need to start practicing law. After that, you have to develop yourself as a lawyer, which goes well beyond anything a law school teaches you and depends on your individual drive, as well as the circumstances and opportunities you find.

There is no way to figure out whether you are truly interested in law as a profession other than to try it. Hearsay doesn't work. When a young lawyer gets out of law school and actually starts practicing law, he or she will know if it is the right career for them. If they are not satisfied, then they will realize they should get out of the profession.

Developing and maintaining skills is key to becoming successful. In terms of the technical practice of the law, I have worked hard to develop my writing skills. I have on several occasions been tutored on speaking skills and oral advocacy. I have learned more about financial accounting and business issues, and I have tried to make sure I spend time with people who have been successful in their own walks of life so I can understand what has made them both successful and interesting to their peers.

Commitment to Working Hard

The best way to learn legal skills is to work really hard. Do it a lot. The more transactions you complete, or the more cases you try, the better you get. The more skilled you become, the more opportunities you will have, and so on in an upward success spiral.

I do not believe practicing law is an endeavor you can do on a limited basis in the hope that your intuition will carry you through. If you look across the board at people who are really successful lawyers and at those people who are leaders in the profession, you will find they are committed, and it shows in their day-to-day priorities. Some people are born with that work ethic and drive. Other people just get into something they really like that gives them a great deal of satisfaction, fueling this drive. And still others simply observe what it has taken for others around them to be leaders in the profession, and they emulate the people they are around.

Preparation is critical to success, and there is no substitute for it. You must always anticipate what will be relevant in a particular matter. Make sure you know both the technical answer and the impact those technical, legal answers can have on either the negotiation of a transaction or the strategy of trial.

I tell young lawyers to make sure this is truly what they want to do with their lives. If it is something they truly enjoy doing, they will likely do it very well and build a great career. However, if they are not genuinely interested, then they ought to find something else to do, because they will not do it very well, and it will be very frustrating for them.

Listening to Clients

The differences between a good lawyer and a great lawyer are judgment and people skills. There is an old saying: "Experience comes from bad judgment, and good judgment comes from experience." You have to stub your toe a little along the way to get that judgment. Gaining people skills is often more natural, but no less critical.

To be persuasive with the clients, you must first listen closely to what is important to them. From there, you then use your training, logic, and experience to give the same priorities to their goals that your client gives. Not many lawyers are good at listening. Again and again, I have seen how ineffective talking can actually be when interacting with a client. And again and again, I have seen listening work.

The bedrock of being a good lawyer is attaining a sound technical knowledge of the law, but to be an exceptional lawyer, you have to apply that expertise together with your own good judgment and an awareness of the client's needs, as well as an understanding of their approach to their unique situation.

The most outstanding lawyers are people who derive a strong sense of satisfaction in taking care of those around them, whether they are clients or colleagues. People who are overly selfish in their approach to life generally don't do very well in a professional services position. A lawyer has to know how to represent a client in terms of their best interest, according to what the client wants, as opposed to the lawyer just making the decision for the client.

The best lawyers always recognize that their success depends on representing their client effectively. Lawyers who don't start with providing quality legal representation as the principal goal end up being less effective in the long run. Success happens when every client you represent thinks you have done a wonderful job.

The Challenges of Life as a Successful Lawyer

Staying on top of the ever-growing body of knowledge is a challenge. As business and law are constantly changing, it is important to have a group of trusted, smart people to talk to and learn from all the time. I particularly talk to the CEOs of other significant organizations about how they deal with the changing world around them. At the same time, I read constantly. I read the *Wall Street Journal*, *Fortune*, *Forbes*, and business newspapers, as well as a variety of books and publications dealing with leading professional service firms and what is going on in the legal profession on a global basis.

Finding balance in your life is also a challenge. It is hard to balance your personal and professional life when being professionally successful means putting so much into your work. It is hard. You just do the best you can and cram as many hours as you can into the day. For me it means getting up very early in the morning on the weekends and working a little to spend time with my family later. There is no set way of doing it, and I think any person who works as hard as you need to work will see that the professional will have to face the issue of work/life balance. My wife is a lawyer, so she understands what I do, but my children have absolutely no interest in entering the field.

In today's modern world, the lawyer plays a mix of roles, although he or she never has enough time to play all of the roles in as in-depth a manner as he or she might want. Lawyers always seem to be pulled in a number of different directions at once. To face these challenges, lawyers find themselves working longer and harder because managing to do a good job in all of these different roles takes a great deal of effort.

Lawyers as Leaders

Every organization needs leaders, and law firms are not different in that respect. Becoming a leader within a law firm partnership is not an easy task, but the path to leadership is logical. Given our professional standards and expectations, as simple as it may sound, the first mandate of leadership in the law must be to do a really good job as a lawyer. Aspiring law firm leaders must first become known for excellence in the profession and establish a track record of helping other people achieve their goals.

To actually realize success, you must give people jobs that play to their particular strengths so that you bring enough talent to bear on every issue you can. This is part of being a strong leader. As a leader, I have learned never to ask anyone to do a job at which I think they are likely to fail.

Leaders in a partnership get a lot of advice on how to do everything. Most lawyers practice in real partnerships, and it is important to maintain the respect and goodwill of your partners. Sometimes it is difficult to politely tell partners who are your peers and friends that maybe their view is not the same as yours. You must create a culture of both collegiality and respect so that people will look forward to helping one another in the same way they look forward to helping their clients. This culture of respect and collegiality has to extend from the lowest employee all the way up to the most senior partner, and must be reflected in how you respond to people in every situation.

I have learned so many things from others I know who have succeeded in what they do. I have been fortunate to be around leaders and successful people. I have learned from these people and from their experiences and successes. I strongly recommend finding and creating friendships and relationships with a broad range of people whose experiences will enrich your life in a very appealing and meaningful way. You will learn a tremendous amount by being around talented and successful people because they have had opportunities to experience so much in life.

The Role of Lawyers in Society

Society must value the benefits we enjoy in this country because of the rule of law, as opposed to a political rule or a rule of dictatorship. The rule of law and transparency of process are keys to our democracy. Society must, by extension, also recognize the lawyer's role in preserving this system in which the rule of law reigns, so that the workings of the government are transparent to the people. To me, being a lawyer means serving clients in an independent manner; this provides the satisfaction of serving others in an intellectually gratifying way. This, I believe, is the primary function of the lawyer. We must all have stability in our daily lives and safety for ourselves, and in the United States, the rule of law is a bastion of preserving this safety and stability.

No matter how noble the law actually is, however, lawyers themselves many times come across negatively. Lawyers seeking publicity or personal gain for themselves, rather than the best outcomes for their clients, inevitably cause some of these negative impressions. Generally, the range of quality and personality you find in any large group of people, such as the American legal profession, is quite broad. Unfortunately, the stereotype in this field, as in many others, tends to emerge from the bottom of the barrel rather than from the top. It seems to me that both now and in the future, when a client needs you and you do a genuinely good job, they are very appreciative. That's success, even though they might be the one telling the next lawyer joke.

Strategies for Success as a Firm

Law firms are, in essence, a group of lawyers who practice law together under the same banner. This simple concept does not, however, adequately address the elements of law firm success. I believe the key to maintaining longstanding success as a partnership of lawyers is the tangible presence of a core firm culture and philosophy – one that members of the firm abide by and are committed to. The presence of a core culture gives professionals a sense of purpose, stability, collegiality, and support. Every decision I make, large and small, on behalf of my firm must be in keeping with the tenets of our core beliefs. To do otherwise risks our opportunity to be a lasting and successful gathering of professionals practicing on behalf of our clients.

Within that framework, however, law firm partnerships must be agile, able to take advantage of change, and must view change as an opportunity for improvement. Change must not be avoided, despite that most lawyers are, as a group, very risk-averse and oriented toward the status quo.

Our firm's strategy for dealing with change is to maintain our core values of integrity and quality of client service, but also to constantly assess how we can improve the delivery of service and the value our clients receive. We never change the core principles that have made us successful, but we are extremely alert to how we can do a better job for our clients. If our internal rate of change is not keeping up with the external rate of change, we are losing ground.

I see a bright future, full of opportunity for lawyers who believe practicing law at the finest and highest level on behalf of their clients is an important endeavor – one worth working hard for. Lawyers who believe this tenet, in my view, will want to practice together with like-minded professionals. Although the specifics of the practice will inevitably change, the guiding principle for success as a lawyer and a firm is a constant – clients first. That is the key.

Walter Driver, Jr., chairman of King & Spalding, focuses on strategic issues, firm growth, cross-office capabilities, and client relationships. He served for eight years in the 1990s as chairman of the firm's Policy Committee.

Mr. Driver's practice has focused on financing transactions, and he has chaired that practice area within the firm. He has been involved with many aspects of representation of financial institutions, including structured transactions, real estate finance, work-out and bankruptcy and banking investigations. He has advised institutional investors in highly leveraged and tax sensitive transactions, working with King & Spalding's tax lawyers in complex cross-border financings. Mr. Driver represents money center banks, regional banks, international banks and large non-bank financial corporations. He coordinates King & Spalding's legal work for financial clients.

Mr. Driver is the vice president and a member of the Executive Committee of the United States Golf Association, having previously served as treasurer and general counsel. He has chaired the Legal Division of the Atlanta United Way and is a member of the Executive Cabinet of the United Way. He serves or has served as a member of the board of directors and executive committees of several civic organizations, including the Commerce Club, Central Atlanta Progress, the Atlanta Chamber of Commerce, Peachtree Golf Club, and the Georgia State Golf Association.

A graduate of Stanford University and the University of Texas School of Law (1970), he joined King & Spalding in 1970 and became a partner in 1976.

MANAGING THE FIRM

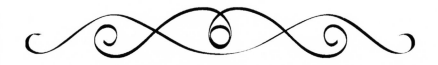

ROBERT E. GILES

Perkins Coie LLP

Firmwide Managing Partner

Creating a Culture

When you manage a law firm, you use many of the same skills in which we were all trained as lawyers. Our firm's philosophy is that there will always be a lawyer involved in the highest levels of management – one who has been an active, successful, practicing lawyer – because that is necessary to make sure you have the respect of the rest of the lawyers in the firm. A successful lawyer has "been there and done that" and knows the concerns partners have with the administrative side of the business. Generally, lawyers don't like to be administered. They don't like to be led, pushed, pulled, or told what to do. They just want to do their own thing. Some of the same attributes that make people good lawyers make them lousy administrators. It is tough to find people who will fill that niche of being a leader or manager of lawyers.

What I try to bring to the job is a very high level of integrity; partners need to trust their managing partner. Many of the decisions I have to make involve either personalities or people's practices. Conflicts are something lawyers get into all the time – not in the personal sense, but in the legal sense. For example, you can't represent clients who have interests adverse to other clients. So when you have a firm as large as ours, you frequently have to make decisions between representing one client or type of client and representing a different client or segment of clients. The reality is that each decision you make on such issues will have an impact on someone's practice. It has been my experience, however, that as long as those decisions are made in a very objective, upfront, and straightforward manner, people trust the decisions are being made in the best interests of the firm and not to coddle favor or friendships.

If your partners trust you, they will support the decisions you make even if they disagree with you. I have seen firms get really hammered by backstabbing and "I told you so" mentalities after a decision was made – always trying to prove the decision was not the right one. We have done a really good job – and this is attributable to our culture and to our lawyers, more than just me – in that if you make a fair decision and if you are very upfront with people about it and get it on the table, even the people who are against it will try to make it work.

I work hard at making sure everyone has an opportunity to provide his or her input on firm issues. My philosophy has always been that if an interested party can provide input before a decision is reached – *i.e.,* if they have the opportunity to influence the decision – then they need to support the final decision and make the best of it even if they disagree. Someone has to make the decision. If you try to manage everything by committee and try to compromise everything, you are totally frozen. I try to facilitate a very fair, straightforward process where people can get their two cents in.

If I am very candid and upfront, and if I truly consider all issues, then most partners feel I have made a judgment as to what is in the best interest of the firm, and even if they are against it, I can't think of any situation where they haven't respected it and moved forward. They don't go out and campaign with others to revisit the issue. Instead, we have a culture of support. Several times we have had a big debate about what direction we should take on a major issue. There were very strong feelings on totally opposite sides of the issue, but once the issue was decided, everyone accepted it and rallied to make it work. Again, I have been at only one firm, so I don't know where it came from, but we have always had a definite culture of open and candid input. We have a lot of very intelligent people, and usually the judgment of the group is a pretty good judgment.

Most of all, I try to make sure all partners have an opportunity to present their perspectives. It is very frustrating to have decisions come down that have a direct impact on you, but that you never had a chance to comment on. We have monthly management meetings with an agenda that goes out to all partners five to seven days before the meeting. In this way, everyone knows what's on the agenda, and everyone has a chance to provide input to the management body who will be meeting on those topics. In that way, we really do have a grassroots approach to providing input, and that is what makes partners feel they truly do have an ownership role.

When I came out of law school 25 years ago, the typical large law firm was 50-100 lawyers, of which almost half were partners. When I joined in 1974, our law firm was considered huge with 47 lawyers. Things have totally changed. Back in those days, if you wanted to have a meeting, all of the partners could meet. We are still a partnership, but we had to evolve from a committee-of-the-whole approach, where everyone really did have a true say in every decision, to a more streamlined management process. We now have several working committees that have fewer members than the number of partners we had 25 years ago. Those members, on a delegated basis, make important decisions on behalf of the firm. The transition into this approach, while still making partners feel they are owners and involved and that their input is important, was a very tough management challenge. It is tough to get broad involvement when your organization is so big.

The real focus over the last few years has been to ensure that people feel a part of the firm. As we opened offices around the country, and, indeed, the world, that challenge has only expanded and increased. Even so, we still try to approach things in the same way. Every year we have a partner retreat that includes partners and spouses. We really try to do a good job of presenting meaningful topics and strategic discussions that everyone has a chance to participate in, but also to have some fun. We spend enough time away from our families, and we feel there is an important bonding process associated with getting partners and spouses together. We really do work to make people feel they are part of the firm. The way law firms are set up, and as large as the largest firms are today, this is a major challenge.

Juggling

As a manager, in comparison to a practicing lawyer, I have to balance my time quite differently. On any day, I have vastly more things on my "to do" list than I did as a practicing lawyer. Also, a practicing lawyer can delegate things to associates and other lawyers when things get busy. But it is easier to delegate legal work than it is to delegate administrative tasks. Our job is to facilitate lawyers practicing law, and we don't want to get our lawyers bogged down with spending hundreds of hours on administrative tasks, so these tasks sometimes pile up on my desk.

As a result, I try to delegate more tasks to non-lawyers. We have hired very qualified people in finance, computer information technology, and in other disciplines that don't need to be managed by a lawyer. For example, we have a professional director of marketing. He happens to be a lawyer, but he doesn't practice – he is a marketing expert.

I can delegate those kinds of functions, but the interpersonal issues with lawyers always make it to my desk, and are a big component of the things I can't delegate and *must* do. You have to learn to prioritize your time and be very efficient. I do a tremendous amount of internal communication by voice mail and e-mail. Ten years ago voice mail dominated. Today e-mail has zoomed by voice mail, but either medium is a very efficient way to keep in touch. I let every partner know he or she has access to me. It isn't really a boss relationship – we are all partners, but I have the management job right now. Someone has to do it.

One of my partners once compared running a law firm to running a shopping center. The person running the shopping center has to keep the snow shoveled, keep the trains running, keep the doors open, and make sure the lights and utilities are available. He must deal with all of the things the storeowners don't even want to think about. The store owners just want to come in and assume that the doors will open on time, the customers will be around, and everything will be working.

Running a law firm is similar. I make sure we allocate resources correctly, that we get cases to the right people, and that we make it as easy as possible to make all of the administrative things happen. Still, there are a lot of people issues involved, and I must find the time to make sure my partners know I am interested in their issues and that I devote the necessary time to them. I get a lot of issues in a day, and some are more important than the others, but to the person who is bringing up the issue, that's their big issue. It's bothering them, and I have to find the time to solve that problem. I try not to let things disappear into a black hole because that is the last thing lawyers want. I have to maintain credibility. If I tell them I'll get back to them in three days, I do.

As a managing partner, I am also somewhat of an orchestra conductor. I try to stay on top of a ton of things – for example, information technology. A couple of years ago Blackberry was a new idea, and now everyone has to have one. I try to acquire some basic knowledge about many of those kinds of things. I can't become an expert at everything. It goes back to the concept of delegating. Even though I feel I am pretty good at juggling balls, there are just too many balls in the air.

No managing partner can be fully aware of all aspects of this business. I had a better background than many because I was a business lawyer with a business school degree. We have committees ranging from budgeting to technology. And while I am on most of these committees, there are other people chairing them, and I want them and their staff to really stay on top of things. I try to pick things up through the committee reports and meetings, and from there I try to throw my two cents in. (Some of my partners would say four cents.)

I focus on the law firm management side because that is what I know. I try to attend a meaningful continuing legal education program that focuses on law firm management issues at least every other year. Typically, a couple of organizations have a two- or three-day seminar. These seminars are good for two reasons. First, you hear some excellent speakers and get ideas on how other firms do things. Second, you meet other people who have similar responsibilities, so you learn your problems are commonplace. They are in no way unique to you.

I have also found it helpful to attend executive education programs, which are held at various business schools around the country. I went to a one-week program at the University of Virginia, which dealt with managing change. Obviously, a lot has changed in our firm over the years. And while I attended the program about ten years ago, I learned valuable lessons still applicable today.

I have also become acquainted with a number of managing partners around the country with whom I try to talk occasionally to exchange ideas and thoughts.

Addressing Challenges and Taking Risks

The most challenging part of my job is dealing with partners whose practices have declined, and this has increased during the recent recession. Lawyers like to be busy. When the workload is up, complaints are down, and vice versa. When people don't have enough to do, they are fretting about something and want an outlet for their complaints. You always have ebb and flow, and some people are down, and you can deal with that. But this recession has been a tough one. It has been a year and a half, especially on the business side, where business has been down, and it is very frustrating to the lawyers involved.

A partnership is different than a large corporation with shareholders that have invested. Here, the partners are all owners. As many firms do, we have a merit-based compensation system and a committee that looks at people's contributions and allocates compensation accordingly. When you have a down market – which we haven't had for about ten years, so we have a fair number of people who have never seen a bad market – it is a very difficult thing to deal with. Again, I take the long view. I have been through about three of these, and they seem to occur about every ten years. It is tough for people when they are working very hard, trying their best, and they are very good lawyers, but the work is down through no fault of their own.

It becomes a challenge. I try to motivate and encourage, but to also make sure partners realize that in a partnership that allocates profits each year based on merit and contribution, a reduced contribution will have an impact on compensation. And while this doesn't happen very often, occasionally, it could have an impact on their future with the firm. A partner has an obligation to rebuild a faltering practice. A practice can disappear for a number of reasons, *e.g.,* if a client is acquired or goes out of business. It is a totally different world out there today than it was three years ago. Then it was a classic seller's market, where there was far more demand for legal services than there were lawyers. Now it is a classic buyer's market, where there is an excess of lawyers.

A law firm is a business, and as other businesses do, it is very important for us to evaluate and consider taking appropriate business risks. To grow and prosper in business, some risk is necessary. Today's business environment is a good example. There are opportunities in the marketplace because firms are experiencing significant difficulties. We have obviously tightened our belt and have had a sharp pencil on the expense budget. We recognized and advised all our personnel that our business practice will be affected by the recession and that, as a result, we will have to be more conservative on the expenditure side. Again, we know this slowdown will be over in the next six, 12, 18 months, but for now, we have to deal with it. You have to deal with the hand you are dealt, and this is the hand we have right now, so I encourage everyone to be cautious.

At the same time, there will be – and, in the last year or so, there have been – some unique opportunities. We know our financial strength and our situation are much more stable and stronger than those of many other firms. Some boutiques were very focused on a narrow segment of the market that has just disappeared. In many cases, however, these boutiques had some very good talent. We may be able to attract talent today who were not interested in even talking with us two years ago. We need to take advantage of some of those opportunities.

Again, I think we have a great culture and a great firm. People who work here like it here. We have had very few partners leave for other law firms over the years – a very small handful. Especially in the last couple of years, more lawyers left to join clients because of the allure of stock options. Well, that allure is on the wane, one might say. We have had people who left and have now come back, which I consider the ultimate compliment. Partners like it here. They feel good about their time here.

I really push our partners to take appropriate risks. Lawyers are extremely conservative. The same lawyers who can be very aggressive on behalf of their clients as they take positions, in a business negotiation or in court, are exceptionally conservative when it comes to their own business. I attribute this conservatism to law school training to focus on precedent. We are taught to always look into the past and find the closest similar situation. We look for places where a fact pattern has occurred before. Lawyers want precedent. However, not all opportunities fit into those nice little boxes – most of the time, they don't.

I often feel my job is pushing to make sure we take advantage of, or at least look at, opportunities that are outside the box. The current recession is not the time for us to stick our heads in the sand and feel sorry for ourselves. We have a strong financial foundation, and this is the time to take advantage of opportunities and to expand and strengthen our presence in selective practice areas and markets where we can benefit over the long term. Despite business being tough, we have grown in the last few years by taking advantage of the opportunities afforded us.

Focusing on Client Service

We spend a lot of time emphasizing service to clients. By that we mean not just quality, but timeliness and efficiency. We try to structure ourselves to maximize our ability to provide topnotch service. Law firms differ from a profitability standpoint. It would be great for profitability if you could have ten partners and 5,000 associates, but that is typically not what the client wants to pay for. They want experienced people. We find that using the right mix of experienced people usually keeps a client's bill lower rather than higher. Our ratio of associates to partners is lower than that of many larger firms, and we feel this allows us to provide clients the right mix of experienced partners and associates. As a result, the client gets better overall quality, more partner involvement, and a more reasonable total bill.

To improve communication with clients, we have really moved toward e-mail. It is quicker and cheaper, and it distributes information in a timely manner. In our client relations group, we always have someone dedicated to client updates. For example, when a new bill is passed or a new decision announced that may affect our clients, we immediately e-mail information to an appropriate list of clients who have an interest in those types of issues. We have found e-mail is a much quicker way of getting relevant information in front of our clients. The feedback has been great. Even production is easier and a lot quicker with e-mail. When generating hard copies, you have to deal with what your hard copy looks like, colors, and so on. E-mail is becoming our primary means of communication.

Within the firm, I use both e-mail and voice mail extensively. I issue regular reports and memos. Once a month we distribute the management meeting agenda by e-mail. At the same time I send that out, I will send voice mail to all partners, reviewing the agenda and giving them some more background. It is the same type of report that I might give at the meeting itself, but this gives partners some extra time to provide input on the topic.

Another program that is unique to our firm, although I think more firms are starting to do it, is a client-service interview program. We interview our major clients every year or two and ask them how we are doing. The interviewers are usually the lawyer who is most responsible for working with that client, maybe one other lawyer who is not significantly involved with the client, and me. We cover a number of issues, ranging from the quality of our substantive advice to our efficiency and timeliness, as well as more administrative issues such as billing, and returning phone calls. It is a very efficient means of helping us stay in touch with our clients – a "finger on the pulse" approach.

We even use these meetings to get specific feedback on specific people. Sometimes it isn't a question so much of quality of work, but more of a personality issue. People's personalities mesh in different manners. We have all met people who are very fine people, but we felt no chemistry with them. The same phenomenon applies to lawyers. Servicing some clients is very much a one-on-one relationship, and you don't always hit it off right. So we do the best we can to make sure the primary relationship is working, and we change it where appropriate.

If we have a vision as a law firm, it is to provide quality service at efficient prices and to really wow clients with client service. We get a lot of positive comments that we do a very good job of achieving these goals.

It is a little bit different within the firm. My job as manager of the law firm is both to make sure we are wowing the external client, but also to make our lawyers and staff feel they are part of a firm with a common approach. We consider our culture and the respect with which we treat each other and how we go about interacting with each other, to be a critical part of our success. It all fits together, and that is why people don't leave. People enjoy working here. Even the people who go on to other things speak fondly about their time here.

If people are happy and want to be here, they will do a better job for clients. This goes for lawyers and staff. I meet with all staff in all offices once every 12 to 18 months and give a mini "state of the firm" address. I participate in a rewards program for long-term service. We have all sorts of recognition for long-term employees because we feel continuity among employees is an important element of the service a firm provides its clients.

Law School and the Successful Lawyer

A lot of talented people go to top law schools. A larger percentage of students at the top law schools probably have more of the attributes necessary to be good lawyers. But then the correlation stops. We have a number of lawyers who didn't attend what would generally be considered top-tier law schools, but they still have the personalities and the skills to excel – and they have. So we try to stay very open-minded. We feel that hiring the best associates is the lifeblood of the firm. You have to continue to bring in the very best people as beginning associates so that those associates can move up through the system and strengthen the firm in the long run. If you ever make the decision to stop hiring the highest-caliber associates, you may not see the change in the first year or so, but within a few years, we believe you'd start seeing a definite adverse impact from such a decision.

We have a very strong belief in hiring the best people. We interview nationally. Just because of the cost and time of interviewing and identifying candidates, it's very unusual for us to go to what is considered a second- or third-tier law school in another part of the country from where the office conducting the interview is located. For our Seattle needs, we regularly interview at Washington, Stanford, Boalt, Harvard, Michigan, Virginia, Georgetown, the University of Chicago, and a lot of other top law schools. However, each of our offices will also interview local law schools with lesser reputations, and we have had some very fine lawyers from these schools. Our standards for the initial interview are probably higher at these local schools. For example, we may focus on the top 5 to 10 percent at a second- or third-tier law school; whereas, we might be pretty comfortable with a higher percentage of Harvard students.

We have learned that someone who excels at a lower-tier law school probably has a greater chance of success than someone who did not perform well at a first-tier law school. There are all sorts of reasons people go to different schools, including financial or geographic constraints or lack of focus in college. I always encourage our hiring committee to go behind the resume and look for the other attributes and extra drive that will make a successful lawyer.

Looking into the Future

It is very hard to look into the future in the legal industry. So many things change almost on a year-to-year basis. Seven or eight years ago, who would have predicted the dot-com phenomenon? And three years ago, the dot-com collapse? Right now, corporate governance is a huge issue. After Enron and WorldCom and everything that has flowed out of those situations, there has been a tremendous interest in clamping down on corporate misdeeds. There is a real distrust of business that, combined with 9/11 and the general economic downturn, has accentuated and extended the current recession. In the next couple of years, corporate governance will be of great interest. Getting out of the recession – and making the transition from the shortage of lawyers in 1999 to a glut of lawyers today – will be the biggest business issue facing most law firms. Things will turn around, but a firm's financial strength will determine its ability to survive this downturn.

Robert E. Giles is the firmwide managing partner of Perkins Coie LLP in Seattle, Washington. The areas of emphasis in his practice are partnerships, tax planning, real estate syndications, and general corporate practice.

Listed in The Best Lawyers in America and "Washington's Super Lawyers" (Washington Law and Politics, 2002), Mr. Giles is a frequent speaker on partnerships to bar association groups in Washington and a contributing author to Washington Partnership Law and Practice Handbook. His professional and civic activities include serving on the boards of directors of Junior Achievement of Puget Sound, the Sports & Events Council of King County, and the Chief Seattle Council of the Boy Scouts of America. He also serves on the board of trustees of the Greater Seattle Chamber of Commerce.

Mr. Giles earned his BA, summa cum laude, and his JD at the University of Washington.

CHALLENGES AND RISKS IN BUILDING A LEGAL PRACTICE

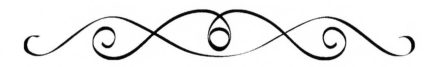

BRYAN L. GOOLSBY

Locke Liddell & Sapp LLP

Managing Partner

The Art of Being a Good Lawyer

Simply stated, the key factor in being perceived as a "good lawyer" by your clients is being recognized as bringing value to their business through focused expertise and outstanding service. To be considered a "good lawyer" in a law firm, you must be focused on the fundamentals of your practice – not only developing a reputation for expertise and top-quality work, but also developing the skills to have a rapport with your colleagues and clients. If you develop a reputation for doing your work right, doing it fast, and doing it with integrity, your productivity, your compensation, and ultimately your success will naturally follow. There are no shortcuts to success in any service business, particularly the business of providing legal services.

Many new lawyers don't understand that the practice of law is not only a business, but it is primarily a "people business." To succeed in this business, you must not only communicate with your clients, but also interact with them in a manner that makes them recognize that you have unique expertise and that your interests are aligned with theirs. This perception is critical so that your clients don't view your legal services as a commodity. Being viewed as a commodity can result in a client comparing your rate and services with those of other lawyers, as opposed to appreciating the particular value you bring to a given transaction or matter. The art of being a good lawyer is being able to distinguish yourself from other lawyers through more than just technical ability.

The difficulty for law firms in recruiting attorneys out of law school is the inability to accurately gauge the intangible qualities of a potential lawyer. While most firms focus on a candidate's academic record, this is only an indication of how good a lawyer may ultimately be from a technical standpoint. Without question, if you're not a good technical lawyer, it's hard to become successful. But technical skills are only a small part of the equation necessary for success. If you cannot translate that technical ability into a client's feeling of confidence, it will be difficult to be rewarded by that client for the value you may be bringing to his matters. To some extent, the difference is not how good a job you did, but how good a job your client thinks you did. Marketing your expertise and your results to a client are not skills taught in law school, and it's something many lawyers have difficulty mastering. How a client perceives value is a key ingredient in any attorney's success.

A law firm's total performance is based on its attorneys performing high-quality work and being paid appropriately for those services. The challenge is not only delivering a high-quality product to a client, but also giving that client an incentive to send you additional work in the future. Assuming a quality result, service may be the determining factor in getting additional business.

In law school, time is your friend, and you can, if necessary, stay up all night to study for a test. Time is your enemy when you're a lawyer. You often do not have the luxury to devote an infinite number of hours to a particular project. Multi-tasking is essential. You have to be able to work on a variety of different projects at one time without affecting a client's perception of the importance of their particular project. Even though your workload may be overwhelming, you cannot afford to let it affect the quality of your work or your service levels. The ability to perform numerous tasks efficiently it not so much a strategy but a requirement.

Advice for Lawyers

The best legal advice for new lawyers is that they should develop a relationship with their clients and be viewed as a partner with them on addressing their issues, as opposed to being merely a seller of legal services reacting to their issues. It sounds simple, but it's not. Developing these types of client relationships will set you apart from your peer group and your legal competition. Developing a loyal and productive client base merely by displaying your superior technical skills as a lawyer or using the institutional branding of your law firm is difficult. It is important to develop a personal relationship with your clients – not so much by being a friend (although that often helps) as by being viewed as invested and aligned with them on their problems and issues. These are the types of client relationships you can build on over the long term.

No client will gladly pay you your billing rate unless you're delivering perceived value to their business. This requires you to stay as involved as you can in industry conferences, keep up to date on what your clients are doing in a particular area, stay abreast of current issues, and provide meaningful involvement in your clients' matters. You also need to be aware of the day-to-day operations of the client and their business. It's difficult to give quality counsel if you don't know what your client is doing on a day-to-day basis. The best legal advice is given within the parameters of known business facts and strategy, and it is necessarily a mixture of legal and business advice.

A key ingredient for client satisfaction is to provide clarity of communication regarding the cost and expertise involved for a particular service. For example, in most cases, though I am the point person for the clients I represent, I may also have two or three other lawyers available, as well. Clients typically contact either me or another member of the team, knowing we will get back to them very quickly. We are in a service business; we should return calls and respond to our clients as quickly as possible. Our goal is to make our clients feel we are attuned to their business and their problems. Quick service is an important way to express that alignment, and in the end it leads to a more productive attorney-client relationship.

Being a Partner: The Challenges of Leadership

For a lawyer fresh out of law school, a law firm is primarily interested in whether you're doing good work and whether you're sufficiently productive to the firm. As you move forward and become more established in your career, the challenge is being a top lawyer who can attract new business to the firm. That means either attracting brand new clients to the firm or attracting new lines of business from existing clients. This type of marketing of yourself and the firm is a challenge to all young lawyers. It is apparent that law schools do not teach students to be successful marketers of legal services, although in the real world of selling legal services, it is a necessary talent.

In our firm, we have a seven-and-a-half-year partnership track, which allows qualified candidates to move directly into equity status with the firm. We're looking for the total package in a partner candidate – one who produces top-quality work and also shows the people skills to develop a quality practice. Our firm is in the business of developing top-quality partners. We don't really have a quota for the number of attorneys eligible to make partner in a given year. The size of the partnership class is somewhat irrelevant, as long as we're bringing in qualified candidates. Our success or failure as a firm will ultimately be based on our ability to develop outstanding partners.

Unlike a corporation, a law firm essentially has a horizontal organizational structure with many partners who are essentially on the same level. The managing partner works with the management committee to determine policy and make certain day-to-day decisions. It's a very flat organization, requiring more interaction with people on the same level than in a normal corporate environment. Day to day, the difficulty for me as managing partner lies in achieving the right balance between being productive in representing my clients and still attending to firm business. Managing a firm requires the same type of focus and approach that being a successful lawyer requires. The challenge is that to stay effectively productive with the clientele I represent, I must continue to focus on the development of additional business.

The most difficult and thankless part of the job is making the tough calls, such as deciding partner compensation, providing input on who makes partner, and, invariably, dealing with people who are not experiencing success for whatever reason. Sometimes you have to make difficult choices that are in the best interest of the law firm franchise to ensure the stability and attractiveness of the firm over the long term.

Assessing Risk

When defining your business risks, you need to analyze the moving parts of your business and what drives your revenue. There are really only two major fundamental components of success. First, a law firm must maintain and add top-quality clients (who in my view are, for the most part, national clients with very sophisticated legal work). This allows attorneys to work on interesting matters requiring valued expertise. Second, a firm must attract top-quality lawyers, either out of law school, through the lateral attorney market, or through the acquisition of additional groups of lawyers, either within a firm's existing markets or in new markets. This is all with the objective of driving revenues. Every law firm must grow its revenue base to remain competitive in the legal market and compensate its people accordingly. Increasing the number of lawyers, raising billing rates, moving into more lucrative practices, and eliminating non-lucrative practice areas are necessary aspects of law firm growth. A law firm must be constantly attuned to the risks it undertakes to satisfy these growth objectives.

Our firm did not, for example, move as aggressively into the technology area – particularly emerging company technology – as did many other firms over the recent years. While we wanted a growing technology practice, we also wanted to maintain our diversified client base. We did not over-commit to this industry for two simple reasons: First, it's very competitive, and second, a significant number of these potential clients are unable to pay for legal services as performed. That is why a number of law firms took equity positions in those companies in lieu of fees. The only way a law firm would ultimately get paid by this type of client is through a financial transaction that would allow them to pay off outstanding legal fees through, for example, an IPO or an institutional funding. To the extent equity positions were used as payment, value would be received based only on some type of monetization of the position. Many firms were negatively affected if they were heavily involved in representing those kinds of companies.

We have tried to stay extremely diversified with our client base, in terms of both old- and new-economy companies – real estate, oil and gas, or financial institutions. While we do have a fair number of technology and telecommunications clients, we believe the allocation is prudent. Diversification of client base, much like our 401(k) accounts, is critical to a law firm for stability of growth with minimal risk.

When we are hiring laterally and bringing in new associates out of law school, we try to minimize our risk by targeting the top students from the top schools, which we believe increases our chances of success. Our firm is still in its entrepreneurial growth stage, and we view our associates not as employees but as potential partners. It's very important that we bring in top-quality people we feel will have the opportunity, should they want to build their own practices, to become top-quality partners in the firm. We also look at lateral partners and try to identify the risks within their particular practices – whether they will be able to deliver business if they join our firm, and whether they will be productive lawyers within our system. We have a working partnership, and it is important that all of our lawyers be individually productive in servicing our clients.

To facilitate our representation of national clients, we need to continually consider new markets. Before opening a new office, it is important to assess the risks and understand the market. You must have high-quality lawyers on the ground with a sustainable, quality client base in that market to minimize your risks. Many firms have not adequately assessed those issues, and they have suffered as a result. The likelihood that you will be a market leader outside your home markets is low. New markets can be very risky and, if they are not prudently underwritten, can end up being a drain on your partnership performance, which can dramatically affect partner profits and, ultimately, the stability of the organization.

The Changing Legal Profession

Without question, the biggest change we've seen in the legal profession lately is the renewed focus on the role of lawyers in representing public companies and their boards in the post-Enron environment. Sarbanes-Oxley, together with proposed federal regulations and stock exchange requirements, is requiring the legal profession to reassess lawyers' duties to public companies, their boards, and the public at large. The emphasis on corporate governance will require a continual reassessment of our role as lawyers and our duties to our clients.

Disclosure issues have and will become much more problematic and complex as lawyers must determine whether clients are appropriately making lawful disclosure based on all the facts and circumstances in this new regulatory environment. This new "watchdog" role may prove problematic as lawyers struggle with these new duties in the confines of the relatively limited flow of information by large public companies to their outside counsel (which may include many firms), coupled with the traditional attorney-client privilege issues. Although these recent changes were made in good faith in response to very troublesome corporate developments, we may end up with a scheme with excessive regulations that could negatively affect corporate America and the economy as a whole.

Bryan L. Goolsby, managing partner of Locke Lidell & Saap LLP, practices corporate and securities law. His experience includes representing corporations and underwriters in public and private offerings of debt and equity securities, representing purchasers and sellers of both public and private entities, and advising and representing boards and board committees. He is also active in legislative matters on behalf of certain industry groups.

Mr. Goolsby holds a JD, with honors, from The University of Texas School of Law. He received a Bachelor of Business Administration degree in accounting, with honors, from Texas Tech University in 1973.

THE ADVANTAGE OF FOCUS

ROBERT F. RUYAK

Howrey Simon Arnold & White LLP

Managing Partner and Chief Executive Officer

The Art of Litigation

If you concentrate on litigation and trial work, as I have, the "art" is understanding how people think, how they react, and how they use their life experiences to make decisions. The entire goal of a trial is to persuade a jury or a judge that your client's position justifies their decision in your favor. If you have a sense of how people think and how they operate, you are more likely to be able to persuade them.

There are several characteristics of successful trial lawyers. The first one we have just addressed – understanding how people think, feel, and operate. You must have good judgment about human nature – not just any human nature, but the particular nature you are dealing with. Judges are often very different from jurors, for example.

Second is the ability to tackle and master new and unfamiliar information. The ability to synthesize and use complex facts to persuade your audience can vary dramatically in terms of difficulty, depending on what kind of case you're working on. Having a complete command of the facts will be persuasive. Most people – most

Americans, at least – are persuaded by the facts and the circumstances that they learn or infer from a particular argument or position. The facts can include the documents involved, oral historical detail, and the people and personalities involved. Some of the best trial lawyers can almost block out nearly everything else and absorb enormous amounts of information in a very short period of time, and then synthesize it and play it back in a way that is understandable and persuasive. You cannot be superficial; you must have depth and breadth in your understanding of the subject matter. Being persuasive is not simply spouting off favorable facts. Persuasion is confronting what your opposition or a witness says by taking individual witnesses' testimony and documenting evidence and putting it together in a form that is convincing.

The third characteristic is simply a broad life experience. Some of the best trial lawyers I've met are people who have had a variety of experiences. They've had the opportunity to work with different types of people from different economic and social levels. When you do that, you have a better understanding of how people think, react, and feel. Armed with that knowledge, they understand the appropriate way – indeed, the persuasive way – to approach their audiences.

Organization is the fourth essential ingredient of success. You need to arrange the evidence that proves your client's position in an organized fashion. Juries use common sense as a principle method of evaluating what they see and hear. That does not require being pedantic or practicing law in a textbook way. It means being able to sense what is important, choosing your issues wisely and supporting your position with facts organized in a deductive sequence – one that a judge or jury is most likely to understand and agree with.

Success is not likely without the fifth characteristic: time commitment. Achieving success as a trial lawyer requires an extraordinary amount of time and an intense concentration on the case. You need to have a great deal of patience and be willing to be consumed by the facts. Most people are convinced when they believe that the speaker knows what he is talking about. You must convince the fact-finders that you have complete command of the facts and have thoroughly analyzed them, and that your arguments are not conjectural, but are the true and proper conclusions.

The Changing Face of Law

There have been significant changes in the practice of law in the last few years. Procedurally, one major change has been the courts' adoption of methods to accelerate litigation and get cases to trial more expeditiously. New procedures to resolve discovery issues, early disclosure requirements, limitations on discovery, and time limits are all in vogue today.

There has also been continuous change in specific areas of law in the last five to seven years. These changes will affect how you prepare a case and are particularly significant for litigation. The sheer number of cases being decided has made it difficult to keep up with all the changes. Just as in the information age we find ourselves deluged with information, in the legal area we are deluged with new case law. This problem intensifies daily. It can be difficult to stay on top of it. That's one reason we have made a decision, as a law firm, to focus our practice on three specific areas: antitrust, intellectual property, and complex litigation. We are not a general practice firm. The benefit of this focus is the ability to develop a deeper and broader capability in those specific areas of law.

Staying on top of new developments is challenging. One mechanism we have in place helps. We have 20 to 30 trials a year in the firm, and we often have attorneys, economists, and staff who have tried the case hold review sessions. Like surgeons on grand rounds at a hospital, we discuss the case – what went right, what went wrong, and what we learned. It's open for anyone who wants to participate.

Our system of knowledge management also provides a great way to develop the knowledge base of the firm. Through e-mail and other means, we constantly stay on top of changes in the law and procedure. It's the responsibility of our three major practice groups to track developments and distribute the information to everyone by e-mail and in writing. It's also important that we get this information to our clients, so our system includes a method of collecting and disseminating such information beyond the firm to our clients, on a routine basis.

Technology has dramatically changed the legal profession. Computer technology has made it possible to increase the speed with which cases can be developed. The Internet has provided dramatically more information to consider. We have a group of very strong, talented people to keep up with changes in technology. Our IT department provides the resources we need to stay on top of technological developments that can be used in and out of the courtroom. We try to make sure we have all of these resources available, particularly in the courtroom setting, where we take pride in being "state of the art" in presenting information at trial. We have a whole team of "roadies" that set up and wire courtrooms and temporary trial offices all over the country.

Challenges of Being a Lawyer

The successful practice of law is time-intensive; the challenge is managing your time effectively. You have to devote a tremendous amount of time to understanding and capturing what you need to know to be persuasive.

Related to this is the challenge of balancing personal and professional lives. Some people get caught up in the belief that clients and the firm demand all of your time, but I've never subscribed to that view. Many lawyers make the mistake of devoting their entire lives to their practice. Quite frankly, those people are successful only to a point. When they fail, they lose perspective and burn out. The practice of law is a job; it's how you earn your income and provide for your family. But it should not be the primary goal of your life. I've always reminded myself, "You need to be able to walk away from it." I think people have to be prepared to do that. As a practical matter, it requires time management skills and the ability to delegate responsibilities. For me time management is ironclad – I plan my schedule so I have significant personal time with my family, and I don't allow interruptions. Admittedly, being in litigation makes this difficult because judges and clients constantly want your time. But I have always found that if you set limits, people will respect them.

A second challenge is simply dealing with people. In a litigation trial setting, you deal with witnesses and clients with emotional views on the issues – particularly in cases that involve hundreds of millions of dollars. Emotions and sensitivities lie behind the scenes. Witnesses' recollections, judgments, and demeanor can be adversely affected by them. One of the big challenges is being able to deal with personality traits and perspectives. You must gain witnesses' trust, help them recollect, and help them formulate accurate and objective testimony.

A third challenge is case management. With witnesses, attorneys, legal assistants, and support staff, you often have a considerable number of people helping you prepare for trial. Managing the case well, so the team can meet all the deadlines, marshal all the law and the facts, capture the right documents, prepare the key witnesses, and put the puzzle together is a huge challenge.

Climbing to the Top

I'm not sure there's any "best way" to learn legal skills. The professional development of a strong trial lawyer requires a combination of things. Large law firms like ours must have a strong, focused, viable training program. Our firm is 75 percent litigation, and our younger lawyers learn litigation skills in different ways.

First, they work with more experienced people. This requires staffing in such a way that the younger people have an opportunity to learn from those who have already mastered the craft.

Second, we have a partner whose full-time responsibility is to set up programs to train the younger people on all the practical skills, such as legal writing, taking depositions, and dealing with expert witnesses, clients, and the opposition. We also start very early with "boot camp" – our summer program for our prospective new lawyers, second-year law students – a two-week intensive program that teaches them all about litigation.

Third is that the more experienced people in the firm must take an "advisory" interest in the younger people and their skills. That happens in our firm through the existence of a formal advisor review program that allows for feedback to younger lawyers intended to make them more successful. I've often heard that in some of the larger firms, young people spend the first two or three years doing very little skilled work – mostly research and little more. That leads to a deadly result because they are not getting the opportunity to develop the skills that will enable them to be successful. With our advisory program, evaluation process, and assignment process, we try to ensure there will be opportunities for young lawyers to demonstrate and hone their talents.

We use an extensive set of criteria to determine promotion to partner. There are four main categories of those criteria, based largely on performance.

The first is demonstrated talent. In the area of litigation and trial work, for example, this includes a proven ability to stand up in adversarial situations, marshal the facts, argue effectively and confront the opposition's position, instill client confidence, and command the respect of the judge and jury.

Second, the partner candidate must demonstrate that he or she has mastered an ability to write persuasively and effectively and has attained proficiency in substantive law. Most successful lawyers try to concentrate in two or three areas of law.

Third, a lawyer needs to display a strong work ethic. That does not mean simply working hard for billable hours, but working efficiently and working well with other people. If you cannot work well with peers, senior partners, and clients, you will not become partner. You must understand and live by the concept of mutual respect. In other words, "work ethic" has to do with being committed, not just to banging out a product or a solution, but to working effectively and efficiently with others. These things are not easy to calculate, but we always see them in those people who make partner. Teamwork, excellence, commitment, and collaboration – that's what we look for.

Finally, the candidate needs to exhibit leadership. One of the most challenging aspects of being a leader is helping people understand their role in the organization. Success is all about leadership. And a firm must have leadership at all levels. You need people who are willing to take on defined responsibilities and help push the firm forward. In every organization are people who believe their role should be greater than it is. At the same time there are also people who are reluctant to take on a leadership role in the organization. If you can find a suitable combination of strengths and roles for individuals in a firm, you will find success. The young people will feel more comfortable with the organization and sense the cohesiveness of the leadership. This works best when people are willing to put egos aside and are not too concerned about titles. This challenge is unique because law firms are structurally different from corporations, which are typically hierarchical. Partnerships are, instead, peer-based structures. If a firm lacks cohesiveness, the organization will suffer as a result.

The Advantage of Focus

The legal profession and the law firm paradigm are changing dramatically and rapidly. To be successful, you need to be able to accept change and adjust to it, always seeking creative ways to take control of change for your firm. I tell this to everyone I can. More has changed in the last five years in the practice of law than had changed in the previous 15 years. It remains a rapidly changing atmosphere. The number of mergers that have occurred between firms, the number of people moving from one firm to another, the size and scope of firms, are all symptoms of this change. The concentration of lawyers in specific practice and areas of expertise is also a symptom. It is extremely difficult today to have a general practice firm with five to ten lawyers in each of 20 different areas; such a firm will not have the resources and expertise to address major disputes.

To manage today's law firm, you need to be able to provide a structure and a vision that will adapt quickly to change. You need to have a strategy. Much like a corporation, you have to develop a very specific business plan for how to achieve your goals, and you have to execute. That's not what firms are used to. In the past, most lawyers in the management of firms – even the major ones – thought of their role more like driving an aircraft carrier. They were there to keep a large operation on course – manage expenses, hire good people, etc. – and the coast would be clear. That's no longer acceptable. A law firm has to have very specific goals and a management team able to execute those goals. Many law firms thought the recent abnormal bubble of work in the corporate area would never end. All of a sudden it came to a crashing halt. The amount of retrenching going on among law firms now is a result of their lack of coherent strategic plans.

Clients today expect more from firms than they have in the past. Before, clients would latch on to a firm and its lawyers, remaining faithful through thick and thin. The important corporations in this country can no longer live that way. They must apply a reasoned approach to the way they employ lawyers: hire the best, most capable, most knowledgeable, and most successful people in the areas of law affecting them. General counsel's jobs are often at stake if they fail. As a result, law firms are now hired for their expertise and proven abilities – not just for longstanding relationships. The shifts and changes in law firm structures are a reaction to that change. Law firms that do not have the expertise, capability, depth, strength, personnel, talent, and resources to manage a $100 million case should not get the business. If you are going to be in a market that requires preparation and trial of such cases, you have to have all of those components to be competitive. That's a tall order. But major corporations now demand such strengths.

Unlike many other firms, we have had some very specific marketing campaigns to coincide with our strategy and vision. We use advertising, internal promotion, and external promotion. Our newest marketing campaign is called "The Advantage of Focus." The idea is to present ourselves as a large firm that is highly specialized, but with incomparable depth of experience, talent, and resources in our areas of practice. Each of our three areas of law now has about 200 lawyers working in them. With such vast resources, we are able to handle virtually any matter successfully. We have made very strategic personnel acquisitions in those three areas. That is the "advantage" of "focus." I think we've been successful. We are getting surveys ranking us among the top three firms in the world in each of those areas. We can bring four or five lawyers to an important matter who will have a combined 100 years or more of experience in dealing with the clients' specific issues. There will be virtually nothing that one of them hasn't seen before. The advantage of focus is a powerful message and a powerful asset for any client. And it differentiates us from all other firms.

Social Responsibility

Lawyers have a multifaceted role in society. As a result of the power that lawyers wield in developing and enforcing the law, there is a tremendous responsibility to help move the law in the correct way. As a lawyer, your responsibility is to represent a client to the fullest, but also to recognize the inherent limits. You cannot get lost in the job; you need to maintain a standard of ethics and exert leadership to ensure that the rule of law is not compromised. There are restrictive rules, but, more importantly, there must be an understanding within a law firm that you have a positive responsibility to help develop the law in those areas in which we lead. This means devoting time to professional and public service. This means providing time and people to serve temporarily in governmental or public interest positions, in leadership organizations, and in professional advancement roles.

We must encourage and reward such contributions. For example, four of our partners have served as chairs of the Antitrust Sections of the ABA, and many others on a variety of subcommittees. Others have served as temporary special prosecutors and in critical government agency leadership positions. Some others have played a role in the development of interest law and policy in the area of intellectual property and computer law. The truth is that with all of the talent and expertise available in the firm, there must be a commitment to use some of it to advance the profession, our system of justice, and the law itself.

On the other end of the spectrum of social responsibility, we also concentrate very heavily on providing services to those who cannot afford them. We work with our local organizations on *pro bono* work in the DC Bar and with other legal service organizations in the cities where we are located. We commit 5 percent of our billable work to *pro bono* cases and projects, and we give full billable credit for the time our lawyers spend on these cases. We also take on major cases when the implications are for broad groups of people harmed or disenfranchised. For example, we are currently working on class action cases representing black and Spanish farmers who have for years been cheated by the federal government and crop buyers. We have another case in Montana representing more than 200 homeowners whose property was destroyed due to an improper Forest Service backfire. Major law firms have a responsibility to take on such important cases and use their incredible resources to right such wrongs.

There are, I think, some golden rules for being a lawyer. The first is fairly basic: You cannot overreach; you have to operate within the law. You should contribute to the development of the law and the ethical application of the law.

The second rule is to always operate in the best interests of your client. That means you may need to put some of your own professional goals aside at times. I've seen some lawyers get far too involved in building their own reputation and expertise, often when it is not in the best interests of their clients. An example might be someone going to trial for experience when it is not always in the best interest of their client; they might be able to get the best possible result for their client through settlement.

Third is to always maintain a professional demeanor and character. Arrogance is common in this profession, unfortunately. People who are professionally arrogant hurt themselves and their clients. Develop mutual respect for others, whether they are the opposition, the judges, witnesses, or peers in your law firm, because in that way you are more likely to persuade and be successful.

The law firm, through leadership and policy, must promote and insist on social responsibility by its people. Our firm has a zero-tolerance policy for ethical violations. Taking a hard-line ethical stance is very important; it can be so easy to slip into the "winning at all costs" attitude. I've seen that happen in law firms, and it's extremely detrimental. We also have a zero-tolerance policy for discriminatory or unfair acts and practices. We have to make sure our people are comfortable in their workplace. Beyond these standards, we also contribute charitably as much as we can, including money, time, and effort. We've adopted a public elementary school, where we have our people teach and work with the children and support the school and parents financially and in other ways.

The Future of Law

The law and its application will continue to change very rapidly, becoming more complex and more global in scope. You need a structure in place to deal with such change. One aspect of that structure is a knowledge management system within the firm that links technology and people, so knowledge and information are easily disseminated throughout the firm. The technical infrastructure of the firm must continue to grow and develop to be able to meet the demands of the day. You also need a solid training program for the younger people in the firm, so you can ensure they will develop their knowledge and skills at a faster pace.

The antitrust field is changing. Globalization is here. It's no longer enough, for example, to have a U.S. merger practice; it has to be global. That's why we have opened a Brussels office, and we've acquired more than 15 European lawyers. We have to be prepared as a law firm to provide for our expanded client needs. In intellectual property, as well, there has been a great convergence in the laws in Europe and the U.S., and they increasingly resemble one another. IP rights are now global in dimension and risk. Globalization is also changing the face of dispute resolution. There has been significant growth in all types of litigation and adversarial proceedings. International arbitration is a strong and growing area of law, for good reason: The issues are now international in scope and beyond the jurisdiction of the U.S. court system. The move toward arbitration proceedings – where you can deal with international issues, confrontations, and disputes more successfully – will continue at a very rapid pace.

Areas of law are developing in Europe that were not as important before. For example, environmental issues are on the rise in Europe, as are product liability cases. These issues have required us to expand the scope of our firms' capabilities. The main point of all of this is that the issues our clients will have to face will increase dramatically in size and scope as a result of globalization.

The implications of international law and the increasing number of jurisdictions involved present interesting and serious communication and information requirements. Achieving the client's best interests will mean navigating a variety of languages, distinct cultures, and national and supranational authorities. For example, the European Union has its own structure of regulatory authorities. Staying abreast of all of these new laws and effectively communicating with the various authorities and participants remain difficult tasks.

More than ever before, the leadership within law firms of the future will need to understand the importance of a truly professional structure to manage the firm, create a vision and strategy, and execute tactically. Law firms have too often typically been undisciplined organizations of powerful professionals who make decisions based on the present situation. Growth, for example, too often has been the natural result of current, transient demand. That is no longer effective; they need three-year, five-year, and ten-year plans, and must be able to execute on those plans.

Sometimes that means making hard decisions, such as cutting out a practice group and focusing on those you believe are vital to the future. You will have to be strategic and hire to suit the needs of the future, not just current ones. Success today and in the future will be more a product of careful and innovative business planning and performance than it has been. Competition among firms for the choice employments and clients will become fierce. And profitability and success will be realized by the well-run, efficient firms that will be able to attract, keep, and further develop the most talented professionals. I am confident that, as a firm, we are focused on these goals and are on course.

Robert F. Ruyak is one of his firm's most experienced, successful trial lawyers. He is the managing partner and chief executive officer of Howrey Simon Arnold & White, LLP, and serves as chairman of the firm's Executive Committee.

A partner at Howrey since 1981, Mr. Ruyak has extensive litigation and jury trial experience covering a wide range of commercial disputes and substantive areas of law. He has tried cases in the antitrust, patent, trade secret, insurance coverage, commercial contract, and international trade areas. His experience encompasses matters involving computer hardware, software, telecommunications, semiconductors, medical devices, chemicals, food, steel, paper, transportation, heavy equipment, and automobiles, among others. He specializes in managing and trying complex cases, representing plaintiffs, as well as defendants.

Mr. Ruyak has been at the forefront in advocating and employing innovative evidentiary techniques in jury trials and in promoting corporate-style law firm management. He is a frequent speaker at conferences and seminars addressing the protection and enforcement of intellectual property rights, jury trial strategy and tactics, and the use of technology in litigation.

Mr. Ruyak earned his BA at Gannon University and his JD at Georgetown University Law Center.

THE ROLE OF THE LAWYER IN BUSINESS AND SOCIETY

ROBERT O. LINK, JR.

Cadwalader, Wickersham & Taft

Chairman

Lawyers as Facilitators of Society

Lawyers are primarily facilitators. I come from a corporate transactions and securities background, as opposed to a litigation background, and of course it's important to differentiate between the types of law in practice. There are real dichotomies, especially between transactional attorneys and litigation attorneys.

At my firm, for example, we have a Litigation Department whose mission is to protect our clients' interests in the courts and other forums. We have many other departments, however, such as Capital Markets and Tax, whose work is transactional in nature – *i.e.,* structuring deals for the business advantage of our clients. While a litigator will frequently call upon the expertise of a colleague in a transactional department, and vice versa, the nature of their respective practices is fundamentally different.

Nonetheless, at its essence, the art and the science of law is to act as a facilitator. Good negotiating lawyers facilitate transactions and the ability to do business in the same way litigators facilitate conflict resolution. If you view the laws as rules that govern the conduct of society, then lawyers are facilitators who help society run properly.

Because of the publicity surrounding the unfortunate actions of a few, lawyers are frequently perceived negatively by society in general, but this perception is most often unwarranted. Many of the stereotypes are unfounded and cannot be generalized. The legal profession is a noble one that plays a vital role in society. It provides a dynamic, exciting, challenging career for people and can be very economically rewarding, as well. It's an issue that the bar associations have so far failed to successfully address, and I strongly believe the legal profession should make a concerted effort to improve its public image.

There are certainly aspects of the bar that should be brought to bear. I would love for people to be more accountable for their actions. I think one of the problems with society – and one of the reasons lawyers take so much blame – is that lawyers represent clients and try to fulfill their wishes. We have a very litigious society right now, with too much blame-shifting and people who refuse to take responsibility and be accountable for their own actions. I am a believer in the Constitution, with its parameters that allow for interpretation, but if there were a way to enact a law that would mandate that all people be accountable and responsible, I would be the first to vote for it.

Success as a Lawyer

Everyone's vision of success probably differs because we all aspire to different goals. Goals have to be attainable, realistic, well communicated, balanced and, eventually, achieved. People have to understand what the goals are, buy into them, and understand that they are expected to reach them and then be accountable. It's very important to set goals and standards for ourselves. I expect people to reach their goals. They should want to be the very best at what they do.

To be successful as a lawyer, you need to first understand the law extremely well within your specialty, without exception. In addition, you need to understand the business and markets your clients are involved in. The key is to be able to add value to that business, which involves applying appropriate business judgment. Good lawyers understand the law and work hard, but a great lawyer understands the client's business as well as, if not better than, the client does. A great lawyer understands the market the client operates in and understands how to facilitate and add value to that client. Incorporate the skills you've developed with a sense of optimism and an understanding of the tools of the trade, and be ready to work hard. Successful lawyers work very, very hard.

Finding a balance between your personal and professional lives is one of the greatest challenges you will face in the practice of law. Law is an exciting, dynamic, wonderful profession, but it requires a great deal of time. When you're in a client-service-related business, the needs and expectations of your client and their time schedule have to take precedence over your own. The tug-of-war between your professional and personal lives is difficult, and it's just something you have to work on. You have to prioritize and communicate – and hope you have a very understanding family!

Time management is crucial if you want to be a successful lawyer. If you can prioritize your time fairly well within your day, you will achieve more. Effective delegation is also very important. The most effective strategy I have learned as a leader within the legal community is surrounding myself with talented, dedicated people. If there's one great key to success, I believe it is that. By surrounding yourself with more capable people, you achieve greater success.

Virtues and the Benefit of Experience

It's also very important to have a reputation for honesty and integrity. I think more lawyers should follow rules of good gamesmanship. What you say should always carry the day and be counted on; it should not always have to be in writing. Similarly, reliability is crucial; you must be able to meet your deadlines and any commitments you've made. After you have developed a reputation in these areas, people will realize that if you are making points and raising issues, then they will be viewed as significant and worth addressing. While it's helpful to maintain a sense of humor, it's also very important not to be cavalier: Be serious, don't ever make things up, and don't change your story halfway through. Follow through and deliver on promises.

To win cases, you need to understand the law, use good judgment, be tenacious, and be creative. Developing your skills in any large-firm environment is a training experience. Everything that helps you understand and learn how to relate to people goes into your frame of reference for how you will function in business and legal roles. The skills you develop can be a combination of your family upbringing, your ability to deal and relate with people, and your ability to understand and empathize with other people and their concerns. Those are all good traits to start out with. The training you receive as a practicing lawyer – from the mentors who have helped and worked with you, from your partners, and from your associates – will continue throughout your career. I am still constantly learning new things.

The best business advice for long-term success is to always add value and to make sure people are happy on both sides of a deal. It's something I learned from my father: A good deal has both sides in a transaction leaving happy and feeling well treated. Good business relies on simple principles of integrity, diplomacy, and an ability to persuade. If you have a sound basis in fact and law and have a well-reasoned, well-organized position you can articulate clearly and with conviction, you will be persuasive and successful.

Leading Lawyers

Attending a top law school puts you higher on the ladder in terms of firms and cities where you can interview, and it can create significant networking opportunities, but beyond that, you will rise and fall on your merits and capabilities. To move ahead, you need to stand out as a leading expert. If you want to get noticed, be the best.

To be a leader among lawyers, you need a vision, and you need to be accepted among your peers. Perhaps the first and foremost quality in leading lawyers is a proven track record in your practice; you need to be a successful lawyer. As you gain the respect of your peers, you will naturally gravitate toward leadership roles in a firm. For partners, the expectation is that each will be an example of a commitment to the practice of law that is second to none. If you accept that commitment and strive to be the very best and work with a firm that wants to be the best, you will find this to be a very rewarding profession. Getting to the top is a matter of building a consensus that you are the person who should be responsible for running the business of the practice. All of the leaders I respect have great vision in their particular industries, as well as integrity and open-mindedness about what they're trying to accomplish. They also have a wonderful drive and a tenacity about them that insists upon success.

The toughest part of running a law firm is that the assets of the law firm are its people, and people carry with them their own set of baggage. It can be difficult to motivate people to deal with behavioral issues because all of these assets of the firm that go home every night will come back the next day. By setting an example and by giving people incentives to be efficient and productive, you set standards and goals for accountability. It's all part of effective client service. Clients expect efficiency and timeliness. If you want to succeed in this market, you have to deliver that. We simply reinforce what we think the clients are looking for, and that is top-level service on a timely and efficient basis.

Managing in an economic downturn shouldn't be much different from managing in a strong economy. A lot of what you do to manage effectively during a turbulent market is hopefully already in place through diversified practices. The best approach to a turbulent market is preparation. It really helps to have good planning, forethought, and a long-term view. When you're in a turbulent market, it's important to constantly communicate with your clients, your personnel, and your lawyers. Stay in touch with their needs, understand those markets, understand its effects on your client, and use people with versatile skills to apply the law in new ways in response to the changes.

Changes in the Legal Profession

The world is consolidating, and businesses are going global. The biggest change in the legal community has been the consolidation of clients and the globalization of the business community. Our response to this phenomenon will define much of the future of the legal profession. Lawyers need to respond to the needs of their clients. Thus, the legal community needs to respond to this new consolidation and globalization of business.

There's an international component in much of what we do. Our firm has responded to this need by expanding into London. If we do not become international, we cannot respond to the needs of our client. I think the globalization of law will continue to cause more standardized controlling laws, whether it's in New York, the U.K., or elsewhere. In litigation, we will see tort reform to limit our highly litigious society.

The information technology revolution is also a major factor in the changes in our profession. With the advent of the Internet and the amount of new technology available to us, the dynamics of how we practice have changed and are changing. We have made a tremendous investment in our information technology group so that we can stay on top of these developments. Just as our clients rely on topnotch lawyers, we rely on experts in the technology field. We all read as much as we can, and we rely on additional experts and professionals to keep our firm at the cutting edge of the innovations. There will continue to be an explosion in technology capabilities that will have an impact on law.

The best way to deal with change is to have versatile, talented lawyers. It's a matter of positioning yourself so you're able to attract, recruit, and retain the very best lawyers who will be able to adapt to change, whatever it is. Change is not a bad thing. Change provides opportunity. It makes our lives interesting. It is constantly happening, so you can't shy away from it. Embrace change, but surround yourself with the very best, and they will be able to effectively deal with it, to the benefit of your firm.

Robert O. Link, Jr., is chairman of Cadwalader, Wickersham & Taft and also serves as chair of the Capital Markets Department. He concentrates on mortgage banking, structured finance, and corporate/real estate. His client representations have included the purchase and sale of residential first- and second-mortgage loans (including FHA, VA, conventional and manufactured housing) and commercial and multifamily mortgage loans in whole loan, participation, private placement, and swap transactions. Mr. Link was instrumental in structuring the first FNMA Multifamily SWAP and has also participated in various forms of recourse substitution transactions and revolving credit/commercial paper facilities secured by commercial real estate. His practice includes transactions dealing with FNMA, FHLMC, and GNMA, as well as purchases and sales of mortgage servicing, due diligence reviews of both residential and commercial mortgage loans, and issues concerning state licensing requirements.

Mr. Link has substantial experience representing commercial, multifamily, and residential loan conduits and clients involved in principal and brokered trades of both performing and nonperforming loans from the FHA, the FDIC, and institutional sellers and the resultant retrades or securitization of the mortgage loans or related mortgage properties. He also has extensive experience in warehouse and gestation "REPOS" and financings, as well as revolving credit facilities. Mr. Link also has experience involving real estate partnerships, joint ventures, and syndications, as well as general real estate and real estate workouts.

Mr. Link joined the firm in 1987 and became a partner in 1990. A graduate of the University of Tennessee in 1977 with Highest Honors and a BS in accounting, Mr. Link earned his MBA/JD degrees in 1980 at the University of Tennessee. He is a member of the Order of the Coif, and a multiple recipient of the American Jurisprudence awards.

ON BEING A SUCCESSFUL LAWYER

R. BRUCE MCLEAN

Akin Gump Strauss Hauer & Feld LLP

Chairman

Preservation, Representation, and Passion

Lawyers have two important sets of responsibilities. First, we are responsible for preserving the rule of law. Our system is based on the expectation that lawyers will conduct themselves in an ethical and responsible manner, and with a high degree of integrity. Absent this integrity, our entire system would collapse. Second, we must vigorously represent our clients, as advisors and advocates. Our system of justice demands a high level of advocacy to reach a just result. Balancing these two responsibilities can pose enormous challenges.

Being a successful lawyer is more of an art than a science. All lawyers are grounded in the science of reading and understanding the law, whether it is statutory law or the interpretation of case law. The art is in the application of the law to ambiguous facts and messy circumstances. Whether you are a litigator or a corporate lawyer, you must understand the client's situation, interpret and apply the law to the circumstances that present themselves, and achieve a result that is consistent with your obligations as a lawyer and provides your client with an optimal result.

A successful lawyer combines both the art and the science of being a lawyer. A successful lawyer effectively uses his intelligence, has first-rate communication skills, possesses a high level of motivation, is grounded in a sense of integrity, and exercises sound judgment to achieve the very best results for the client at all times – and enjoys the task, for a lawyer who is passionate about his or her work is a successful one. He or she shows respect for clients, colleagues, and adversaries alike.

Achieving Balance

Maintaining a balance between one's personal and professional lives will always be a challenge. I recall well a time when, as a law student, I spoke with some of our older alumni about the rigors of studying law and the time commitment required. A distinguished alumnus said I would soon learn that the challenges of law school paled in comparison to those that would face me in the professional world. How true that turned out to be.

A law firm places heavy demands on its professionals. We are faced with the competing demands of serving clients, contributing to the management of the firm, and staying abreast of a rapidly changing legal, regulatory, and business environment. When clients entrust you with their most critical matters, the experience can be a heady one. It becomes very easy to put professional interests before personal ones. However, achieving balance between your personal and professional lives is vital. A well-balanced lawyer is ultimately a more effective one.

Company Strategies

Goal-setting is absolutely and critically important to our firm. We set goals and evaluate our progress. We have very specific goals, all directed at our ultimate objective of being one of the world's great law firms. We constantly monitor our progress. We identify our successes as well as our failures, and concentrate our energies on how we can improve. We measure our firm as an institution against these goals regularly.

In addition to evaluating the firm as a whole, we evaluate the goals of our partners and lawyers individually. We have found this to be a very effective means of managing ourselves. Goal-setting, followed by evaluating the achievement of those goals, has contributed greatly to the success we have enjoyed in the last decade.

A critical piece of strategy development is keeping alert to our clients' needs because, in the end, those needs dictate the services we provide. We constantly watch business trends and monitor our clients' business activities. As the pace of the business world continues to accelerate, clients require higher levels of responsiveness and exceptional value for their legal dollars. Our clients' use of professional services is under close scrutiny, particularly in the present troubled economic situation. To be successful, we must be prepared to respond to that.

Efficiency is an enormous part of providing quality client service. For us, it is an absolute matter of survival. Our clients expect it. Technology puts big demands on us to be efficient. We talk regularly about efficiency – how we can do things better and more quickly, how we can use technology effectively, or how we can staff our cases and matters in ways that add real value to our client service.

The law firm model of billing by the hour contains significant incentives to be inefficient. We have to communicate our commitment to efficiency to all of our lawyers so that they are not drawn into the trap of saying, "Let's put a little bit more work on this matter," or "Let's put a few more lawyers on this case," or "Let's run out that last issue." When our clients compare us to other law firms, we want them to believe they are getting good value. It requires discipline to provide efficient services. To achieve that end, we must communicate often the importance of efficiency, and then provide our lawyers with the tools to deliver that efficiency.

As lawyers, we constantly are seeking opportunities to add value to our services. Identifying and then taking advantage of those opportunities is a tricky business. We must try to react to our clients' needs, anticipating not only their present but also their future needs. What will clients need in the course of the next decade from major law firms, and how will these firms provide those services? We must evaluate a complicated network of feedback, and then attempt to discern the best strategy to ensure that our firm continues to be relevant to the needs of our clients.

Another ongoing facet of our strategic planning involves identifying areas that match long-term opportunity with the firm's special skills. We have developed numerous practice areas where we have significant core strength and where we compete with the best law firms in the country. For example, despite the downturn in the economy, we continue to maintain a strong and solid technology practice. Although technology practices are not currently in favor, technology has nevertheless changed our economy forever, and the technology sector will eventually make an economic comeback. In addition, technology now touches virtually every corporation, not just our Internet, telecommunications, hardware, and software clients. Being able to respond to those client needs has been a critical part of our strategy and has involved the creation of a major intellectual property practice.

As a result of long-term planning, we also built a bankruptcy practice in the heyday of the economic growth of the 1990s. Five years ago we decided that, despite the thriving economy, the fundamental economic principle of business cycles had not been repealed and, therefore, the economy would at some point turn south. In anticipation of this, we built a substantial bankruptcy and financial restructuring practice, and have seen our decision rewarded. We suspect financial restructuring will remain a primary service we provide to clients over the next four to five years.

Another part of our strategy that is critically important is our international expansion. We have international offices, and approximately 25 percent of our business is international – an amazing fact, given that this capability did not exist in our firm a decade ago. Part of our strategy – again, to match what our clients were doing – involved developing the ability to facilitate international business transactions at a very high level. Today, this is an integral part of our firm's current service mix.

In any effort to reposition an organization, we must be willing to tolerate a certain level of risk. There has been some measure of risk in the growth strategy we have employed. In the last decade we have more than doubled in size, to approximately 1,000 lawyers. We would not have been able to accomplish that without taking some measure of risk.

Lawyers are risk-averse; it is one of our core traits. We do not take or handle risk well. However, to be aggressive in our business strategy, we have had to take some risk where perhaps others would not. Our instincts have not always been correct. But on balance, our success has come from our willingness to take risks, understand them, and manage them. Risk does have its limits in an organization like ours. We are not willing to take flyers; we do not do long shots; and we are unwilling to risk undermining the fabric of our firm.

Measuring and Building Success

Extremely successful lawyers exist in all areas of legal practice. Such lawyers have certain key characteristics in common, including intelligence, excellent communication skills, a very high degree of motivation to serve their clients well, integrity, and sound judgment.

The ability to relate well to people is critical. Successful lawyers can communicate with people and gain the confidence of not just their clients, but everyone with whom they work.

Judgment is a critical factor that separates a good lawyer from a great one. Many lawyers are intelligent and analytical, and therefore have the ability to gain a thorough understanding of the law. But effectively applying the law to the disorderly and sometimes chaotic world in which we work requires judgment. Sound judgment is born of instinct and the intuitive ability to sift through the various aspects of problems and devise creative solutions. It matures as we gain experience. Sound judgment is vital to study a very complicated problem, make the best decision, and provide the client with the correct advice. Take a look around the country at successful lawyers at every level, and you will notice the one thing all successful lawyers have is absolutely sound, unerring judgment.

A high degree of integrity also is essential. Successful lawyers are those whose word can be trusted and whose representations are true and complete. Lawyers lacking integrity will find this shortcoming will catch up with them. I have seen many great lawyers practice, and every one of them represents the highest standards and ethics in the profession.

In our firm, one of my responsibilities is to create an environment that encourages our lawyers to be great. I look for people in our firm who have the necessary raw talent, and then develop that talent through experience and mentoring. For me, what has worked in this respect is being very clear with our lawyers about what they have to do to excel in our firm and in the profession in general. Our firm has developed something we call our core values, which incorporate excellence, integrity, and commitment to our clients. We talk about our core values on a regular basis to try to set a tone that allows our lawyers to be able to achieve greatness, to achieve real success in practicing law. Success is not measured only by financial gain; being successful means being a respected professional who excels at the craft of practicing law.

To help our lawyers achieve success as we've defined it, we must mentor them. Leading by example is one of the best forms of mentoring. Successful and accomplished lawyers must work with younger lawyers to develop the skills that will be necessary to make these young lawyers great. Mentoring is a vital part of what we do in our firm, and a very important part of how good lawyers get to be great lawyers. It is unusual for a lawyer to become a great lawyer strictly by his or her own instinct, talent, and experience. All great lawyers have mentors.

Some lawyers – whether they'll admit it or not – measure success by the number of clients a person represents and the amount of money he or she can earn. That is a poor measure of success. Certainly, many successful lawyers have a substantial client following and make a great deal of money. Yet far more important than earning a significant income is making a difference for our clients, within the legal system or in society as a whole. This is the true measure of success.

Professional Challenges

The most challenging aspect of my role as chairman is to persuade more than 1,000 lawyers to move in the same direction every day to achieve the same uniformly high standards of quality and excellence in client service. I have dedicated my professional life to undertaking this enormous challenge.

Trying to build consensus in our firm is probably the greatest roadblock to moving forward as a group because lawyers have diverse opinions about almost every issue. I try daily to take people with very passionately held views – which can differ greatly from one person to another – and meld them into a cohesive team with a common objective. The more aggressive and assertive a firm wants to be, both as a firm and as a business institution, the more divergent the opinions become, and the more passionately those opinions will be held. Our firm is admittedly aggressive, so leadership is an enormous challenge.

Within the firm, many points of view compete with each other constantly, such as conflicts of interest among clients, lawyers who want to pursue a certain line of work with a client, and how aggressive the firm wants to be with its own advice. There is a tremendous temptation to reach compromised solutions and try to make everyone happy. The advice I received when I began this job was that if I was always guided by the principle of doing the right thing, everything else would work out. Compromising to keep everyone happy can become the path to making bad decisions that will come back to haunt you. So I try always to focus on doing the right thing in every kind of decision. I have passed that advice along to anyone who will listen.

The other piece of advice I freely give to my colleagues is that we must remember we are a professional services business. All of our assets are human assets. As important as strategy is, we must always remember we deal with human beings, and our job is to bring out the best in those with whom we work. Every time a decision is made, we must consider whether the result will bring out the best in our people.

As professionals, we are all challenged with how we can continue to provide excellence in today's technologically enhanced environment. When we dealt with a client problem 25 years ago, we worked in an environment of collegiality and collaboration. In seeking to solve a client problem, we communed with those of our colleagues who were in the best position to help us to develop a solution. We discussed the problem, interacted with one another, gained the benefit of one another's experience, and then over time came to a conclusion that embodied the advice we would give our client and the course of action we would recommend. Today, because of the rapid pace of the business world and the demands of technology, we have a substantial amount of pressure to provide instantaneous responses. From our desks, we summon the powers of technology to help us meet our clients' demands for instantaneous responses. That has reduced somewhat the opportunity for collegiality and collaboration, as well as the chance to be thoughtful and reflective, that we once enjoyed. To some extent we have traded contemplation and collaboration for efficiency. The goal is to ensure we do not sacrifice excellence along the way.

One of the great challenges to our profession is ensuring that professional legal services are available to all people in our society. Our firm is committed to *pro bono* efforts and providing legal services to those who cannot afford them. This is a tremendous responsibility for our profession. As law practice becomes more and more focused on operating as a business, I fear that we lawyers may lose track of our responsibility to society and to the system of justice. Large law firms face enormous pressures, such as the escalating costs of technology and the ever-increasing cost of maintaining a talent base. Regrettably, these pressures compete with our ability to devote a substantial amount of our time to the representation of clients on a *pro bono* basis.

The District of Columbia Bar, in which I have been active, has focused on this issue for the past 18 months. In Washington, D.C., we have seen a decline in the volume of *pro bono* services that have been provided by major firms. Given that *pro bono* has been a significant part of our tradition in Washington, such a decline, while probably not unusual, is disturbing. Our system of justice and the rule of law do not work unless everyone has access to legal services. In the future, the tension between those who have benefited from all that has made our country great and those who have been denied access to those benefits will continue to radically affect the law.

The Role of Technology

As I mentioned earlier, technology is a double-edged sword. The use we are able to make of technology and the improvement in the level and quality of service we can provide our clients as a result are extraordinary. Tools that were simply unimaginable a decade ago are now at our disposal. The Internet has changed our lives forever. We can gather information online and use that information in providing advice to our clients, or communicate with our clients directly online.

We use technology to our benefit every day in keeping our clients abreast of developments in their areas of business. We efficiently gather information, synthesize and analyze that information, and then provide our work product to our clients electronically. Whether a court has decided a case or Congress has passed a new law or the IRS has announced a new ruling, we use technology to analyze events and communicate their relevance quickly and efficiently to our clients. Technology is invaluable to our clients, and it allows us to serve them more efficiently.

While these are fantastic tools, these benefits come at a high price. Technology has dramatically changed how we do what we do. We must learn to use the technological tools that enable us to improve our service and our work product without significantly depersonalizing the services we offer. We must continue to interact regularly with our clients and provide them with advice based on significant personal reflection and contemplation. It is critical to be wary that technology sacrifices personal interaction on the altar of efficiency. Technology creates expectations, and the expectations are enormous.

We are faced with the dichotomy that is technology every day. We must reinforce within our firm that although technology is a great thing, it must not take the place of personal interaction with either colleagues or clients. We also must remind both our lawyers and ourselves that while we can now communicate with our clients through e-mail and voice mail, our business is a personal one, and e-mail and voice mail cannot take the place of sitting in the room with a client and working through a problem. If we do not focus our lawyers on this regularly, we will greatly diminish the benefits and value we provide.

Technology should not be feared. Rather, we must embrace it, albeit cautiously.

The Future of Law

In the future, the practice of law will be affected by the four major trends that affect the world economy. The first of these is technology. Over the course of the last decade, technology has dramatically changed what we do and how we do it, and will continue to have an equally dramatic effect over the next decade, as well.

Deregulation is the second trend. By deregulation, I mean not only the fall of communism and socialist governments, but also the ebbs and flows of government involvement in business transactions.

The third trend is consolidation. We have seen it in our profession as firms have merged, and we see it all around us with our clients. Every aspect of industry both in America and abroad has consolidated tremendously, a process that has torn apart the generations-old loyalty of clients to their law firms.

The final major trend that will affect law practice is globalization. There is almost no business entity in the U.S. that is not affected by the international world economy. We are becoming increasingly a global economy, and law practice must reflect that reality.

These trends collectively will change the practice of law radically, so that 20 years from now the practice of law will differ greatly from that which we recognize today.

R. Bruce McLean is the chairman of Akin, Gump, Strauss, Hauer & Feld, LLP. Under Mr. McLean's leadership, the firm has grown to rank among the nation's ten largest law firms.

Before assuming the chairmanship of the firm, Mr. McLean spent more than 20 years litigating complex business cases in federal court, particularly those involving federal regulatory programs, energy issues, natural resources law, and antitrust matters. From 1971 to 1973, before entering private practice, he was a lawyer with the Appellate Court Branch of the National Labor Relations Board. While at the Board, Mr. McLean argued more than 30 cases in the federal circuit courts and had primary responsibility for several landmark cases involving the availability of injunctive relief from government action.

Mr. McLean has handled a number of the largest cases ever litigated between American business and the federal *government. He was lead counsel for one of the world's largest petroleum companies in an action that enjoined and overturned the $100 million conclusion of the Crude Oil Entitlements Program implemented by the U.S. Department of Energy. The decision saved the refining industry more than a half-billion dollars.*

Mr. McLean represented several of the world's largest oil companies and a number of small refineries in the litigation and settlement of claims of regulatory violations brought by the U.S. Department of Energy. He has also represented many other Fortune 500 clients in complex litigation. He has had significant experience in alternative dispute resolution, including minitrials, arbitrations, and mediations.

In his role as litigation counsel, Mr. McLean has helped boards of directors analyze the risk of litigation in significant cases requiring board participation in decision-making. He is a frequent speaker on the resolution of complex business disputes.

Mr. McLean chaired the firm's Washington litigation practice group from 1982 to 1994, during which time it grew from eight to more than 60 full-time litigators. He then headed the firmwide litigation practice group, which grew to 170 lawyers during his tenure. Mr. McLean has been a member of the firmwide management committee since 1979.

Mr. McLean received his BA and his JD cum laude from Indiana University in Bloomington. He attended law school on an I.U. School of Law Fellowship, earning membership in the Order of the Coif and serving on the Indiana Law Journal. He has been a member of Indiana University's board of visitors since 1989.

Mr. McLean is a member of the Federal City Council, a non-profit, non-partisan organization dedicated to improving Washington, D.C., by helping local and federal government agencies meet community needs. In 2002 he was appointed to the Georgetown University Law Center's board of visitors.

BEING A SUCCESSFUL LAWYER

JACK H. NUSBAUM

Willkie Farr & Gallagher

Chairman

On Top of Your Game

Part of the art of being a good lawyer is listening to your clients' problems, understanding their goals, and helping them reach those goals. Being fully conversant with the facts and the problem at hand is another part of it – but the most critical issue is being responsive to the clients and making them feel nothing is more important to you than the particular problem you are working on with them.

With regard to the science of being a good lawyer, understanding the legal problem is a good start. If you can spot the issue and understand it, you can then do the research necessary to understand the precedents and how you can apply them in a particular situation. So the science is really understanding the problem, doing the research carefully, and then convincing someone that your side has the better argument, in a courtroom, a merger negotiation, a will contest, or a divorce settlement. It is always the same task: proving your side is more right than wrong. The side with the better command of the facts and the law will always win. That is the scientific part.

Hard work is the most important element in winning a case, but you also need the facts in your favor. More often than not, the facts will dictate the result, but in those instances where the facts are even on both sides – and some cases are like that – then the person who works harder, is more creative and thoughtful, and devotes more time and energy to the case will probably prevail because he or she will have the edge that hard work yields.

To make sure you are on top of your game and that you look like you are on top of the game in the courtroom, the best strategy is to just study the facts and study the law. If you know both and you have them at your fingertips, you will be on top of the game. I do not travel with an entourage or several briefcases. If you take the time beforehand to put the information that is in those boxes into your head, you do not need any of that. You come with a pad, a pencil, and a head.

The most important part of a negotiation is understanding your end game. Before you go into a negotiation, you have to know what is important to you and your client and what is important to your counterpart and his or her client. You have to navigate the channels to allow both sides to achieve most of their objectives, because a successful negotiation is never where you get everything you want and the other side gets nothing. You want to give up what is not important to you, and keep what is important to you. Preparation for that negotiation is every bit as important as the negotiation itself.

I have always found that yellers and screamers are the least effective negotiators. People who speak quietly, forcefully, and intelligently are most effective. Also, talking too much in a negotiation is not good because eventually you become white noise. People who do not talk much, but have something relevant to say when they do, often turn the focus of the meeting toward what they are saying.

Good and great lawyers both have all the skills needed to be successful. Separating good lawyers from great lawyers sometimes has to do with exceptional intellect. Some people are so smart that they stand out from the rest by virtue of their intellect and thought process, but those are few and far between. More often it is the intangibles – the art of being a lawyer, of persuasion, understanding, and being able to convince a third party of the correctness of your position. No matter how strong your case is or how brilliant your mind is, if you cannot translate that brilliance either to the written word or to the oral word in negotiation in oral arguments in a court, you will not be a great lawyer. The really great lawyers can marshal their facts and the law to make a persuasive argument.

What we look for when conducting an interview with a potential new partner starts with their intellect, and their intellect is best judged by their performance in college and law school. That is what they need to get an interview here. Once they get the interview, we try to sense what kind of person they are, what kind of moral fiber they have, what kind of ambition they have, and what their goals are in life. This is not easy to do in a 20-minute interview. You really look for qualities you think will eventually make a great lawyer.

Going to the best schools always gives you a leg up, whether it's the best law school, the best college, or the best engineering school. However, many of the best lawyers did not go to the best law schools. That is only the beginning. You have to take advantage of the education you receive. The element the top law schools provide you – and actually all law schools do if you pay attention – is to teach you how to think like a lawyer. Lawyers are different from artists because artists can be conceptual, and lawyers have to operate within the four corners of the law. Thinking like a lawyer, spotting the issues, and understanding what is important and what is not are some of the key successes that have to be achieved for young lawyers early in their careers, when they are actually doing the legal work. It is really a question of learning to think like a lawyer and then applying that learning to the actual task.

There are so many examples of lawyers who did not go to the top law schools and still succeeded, so it's fair to say law school is only a launching point. The one real difference with going to a lesser-known school is that it is harder to get a job to showcase your skills.

Ethical Code

Lawyers get a bad rap from time to time about what they do; it is imperative that all lawyers conduct themselves ethically. A lawyer has a twofold responsibility. The first is an absolute loyalty to his or her client. The second is a greater loyalty to uphold the rule of law for the world at large. Sometimes those two loyalties are a little tricky to balance, but as long as you behave ethically, you will achieve that balance. That is the most important thing a lawyer can do.

Sometimes clients want to achieve the unachievable. They want to do things that are simply not legally permissible. It is very frustrating to clients and ultimately frustrating to you not to be able to see things through for them. But you cannot help your client do something wrong.

The law business is no different from any other business – the majority of people who practice law are upright citizens and ethical people who want to do the right thing. There will always be some bad apples. That is true in business and accounting, as we are now seeing. I do not get the sense in my years of practice that lawyers are getting any more or less ethical; about the same percentage of lawyers live by the same rules today as I did when I started to practice law, and the small minority who do not is likewise about the same percentage. It's just the nature of the human being.

The negative perception of lawyers is generated by a relative few, rather than the law profession as a whole. As is typical with the vocal minority, the lawyers who bring the outrageous court claims are the most noticed, and it is hard to respect people who bring those claims. Thoughtful people understand that lawyers fulfill a very important role in society because their job is to make order out of chaos and keep the rule of law going for society. Without a rule of law, we would have anarchy.

The Future and Technology

Technology has changed the way law is practiced today. In the old days – and I started practicing before the Xerox machine – we used to have to mimeograph copies of documents, and secretaries used typewriters to type out long agreements. With photocopying, faxes, and e-mails, everything moves at a much faster pace today, and the expectations of your clients in terms of when you will get your work done have become so compressed that in many cases there is a price to pay in terms of diligence, care, and thoughtfulness in actually preparing the documents you are supposed to prepare. The pace of the practice is just so quick. There is no evidence that it will change. You still have the luxury today of saying, "I will be out of pocket for a couple of weeks," but soon enough you will have a handheld computer that will spew out your faxes and e-mails, and you will have to respond on the spot. The downtime and thinking time will continue to diminish.

The pace has accelerated on the M&A side of the practice, as well. The merger business, while it has gone through differences in techniques, remains basically the same. It is like marriages, which were arranged a little differently years ago, but at their core remain the same – they are the merger of two families. M&As merge two businesses, and I do not think there has been a fundamental change in goal, result, or attitude to get there. However, the speed with which one gets there is significantly different, and I think the stakes are somewhat higher today. The mere size of the mergers we deal with is so staggering that it is a little frightening that the clients demand such speed, as the stakes get ever higher. Basically, although the methodology may have changed, and although the electronic wizardry and machinery have changed the pace, at the end of the day in a merger you want an agreement that protects your client; and in a corporate crisis, the directors still want to be told what to do and how to protect the shareholders and themselves. At the core, what we do is what we did when I first started to practice.

The advent of the computer and cyber space has opened up a new area of law that did not exist before. Rules will have to be created to deal with the privacy issues involved with the Internet. The question is whether Internet law will follow non-Internet law, because basically everything that goes on on the Internet to some extent mirrors what went on in the world as we knew it before there was an Internet. A new set of rules will develop over time, and new laws will come when new technology arrives.

Balancing Personal and Professional Lives

Over the years I have learned that what differentiates lawyers is their response to their clients. When a client calls his lawyer, he has a problem with his financial health. Lawyers deal with people's financial heath; doctors deal with people's physical health. When you call your doctor because you have a pain in your side, you do not want a call-back 24 hours later – you want to deal with it now.

People are the same way with their lawyers; they have a pain in their pocket book and want to deal with it immediately. No matter what you are doing or where you are, you take time out to return your phone calls, and if you cannot do so, you have somebody call for you and explain that you are tied up and make sure it will be okay to call back the next day or later that night. If it is not okay to wait, find a way to make that call, because responsiveness is what differentiates the great lawyer from the good lawyer.

We are always on call, much like a doctor. When you get away from the mechanics of the practice of law and into dealing with clients and understanding their needs, it begins to get much closer to the medical profession: Often the best lawyers are psychiatrists practicing without a license.

In part because of the on-call nature of the work, balancing your personal and professional lives must be done very carefully. It is not always easy, particularly for young lawyers. I am fortunate that I can – within limits – manage my schedule, but I do not envy young lawyers today who really cannot do so quite as easily, just as I could not when I was younger. It is part of the price of achieving success.

Including the management aspect of what I do, I spend about ten hours a day on the job – less than I used to spend, and not every day. In the old days I used to spend at least ten hours a day at work every day. All young lawyers have the problem of balancing their personal and professional lives, and basically every young person who is trying to rise in the business or legal world has that issue. So much of it is personal time management. People who are efficient will manage the balance between their two lives much more effectively than will those who are not.

You must recognize that sometimes you simply have to establish your priorities and stick with them. For example, my son is a soccer player, and his varsity high school games were at 4 p.m. on Tuesdays and Fridays. In three years, I think I missed one game. Many times I went to those games, then drove back to the office and worked until midnight. I simply circled from 3 p.m. until 6 p.m. on game days, and the games became a priority. It's similar to something that a wellness instructor at Canyon Ranch said to a group when I was there, which was the most important lesson I ever got in time management. She looked at this group of largely wealthy New Yorkers and asked, "How many of you go to a psychiatrist?" About half the room raised their hands. She then asked, "How many of you miss appointments with your psychiatrists?" Not one hand went up. Then she said, "It's all about priorities. If you put a star next to your psychiatrist's appointment in your calendar and work everything else around it, you will be able to work everything else around that." She compared it to exercise and said that claiming you are too busy simply will not fly. It is the same thing in the practice of law. You may have to work ten or twelve hours a day, but you can pick your ten or twelve hours more often than not, and if you are willing to be flexible with your schedule and efficient with your time, it can be done.

In short, being a successful lawyer involves a lot of hard work and a few simple but important rules:

1. Understand your client's needs.
2. Fulfill your responsibilities promptly and ethically.
3. Have respect for the other side's position.
4. Respect your role in society.
5. Live your life the way you would like your children to live theirs.

Jack H. Nusbaum is a partner in the Corporate and Financial Services Department of Willkie Farr & Gallagher in New York. Mr. Nusbaum is chairman of the firm and leads its mergers and acquisitions practice group. He specializes in mergers and acquisitions, corporate governance and fiduciary duties, and internal investigations. He also regularly advises boards of directors of public companies on issues of fiduciary duty and corporate governance, particularly in the context of change in control transactions.

Mr. Nusbaum's extensive experience counseling public and private companies in acquisitions and divestitures has involved him in many of the most notable U.S. and cross-border transactions of the past two decades.

Mr. Nusbaum is a director of publicly held corporations, including W.R. Berkley Corporation, Neuberger Berman, Inc., Prime Hospitality Corp., Strategic Distribution, Inc., and The Topps Company, Inc. He also serves on the board of directors of Hirschl & Adler Galleries, Inc., and on the board of visitors of Columbia University Law School. He is a trustee of Prep for Prep and The Joseph Collins

Foundation and a member of the New York State and American Bar Associations.

Mr. Nusbaum has spoken at numerous conferences and seminars on various issues, including accounting irregularities, poison pills and other defensive mechanisms, managing board crises, change in control transactions, and the fiduciary duties of officers and directors of public companies.

Mr. Nusbaum received his JD from Columbia Law School and his BS from the Wharton School of the University of Pennsylvania.

ACHIEVING SUCCESS AS A LAWYER: THE KEYS TO A REWARDING CAREER

KEITH W. VAUGHAN

Womble Carlyle Sandridge & Rice, PLLC

Chair, Firm Management Committee

The Lawyer's Meaning of Success

Any effort to address the art and science of being a successful lawyer must begin with a clear understanding of the term "success" as used in the context of attorneys practicing their craft. Much has been written in recent years about the business aspects of practicing law. Concepts such as "leverage," "client and matter profitability," and "commodity work" are as much a part of the vocabulary of attorneys in mid-size and large firms as the familiar legal phrases *"stare decisis"* and *"res ipsa locquitor."* A casual review of today's legal publications might, therefore, prompt the reader to conclude that a "successful lawyer" is one who employs that set of business practices which generates the greatest profit. Although any profession should seek to employ effective business strategies whenever possible, the true measure of an attorney's success has little to do with the financial consequences of a particular matter for the individual attorney.

Success as a lawyer is properly evaluated according to such standards as the quality of the effort expended by the attorney, the extent of the service rendered to the client, the degree of professionalism displayed throughout the life of the transaction or legal proceeding, and the extent to which the attorney uses his talent and skills to serve others. This chapter identifies the characteristics of a successful attorney as measured by these criteria and concludes with additional suggestions for those who wish to be successful practitioners in a mid-size or large firm.

Characteristics of a Successful Lawyer

Commitment to Client Service

All successful attorneys have one characteristic in common: They are absolutely committed to client service. They may come from different law schools. They may have chosen to specialize in different areas of practice. They may vary in legal knowledge and skills. They may differ in age, gender, race, religion, or background. But, in the final analysis, all are devoted to their clients and are motivated by an overwhelming desire to serve their clients' interests. The flipside is also true. Highly skilled attorneys who are not committed to serving their clients will achieve only temporary success at best. As one of my partners said recently, "Clients don't care what you know until they know that you care." The importance of this factor is not surprising when you remember that lawyers are in the business of providing professional (in our case, legal) services. The use of legal knowledge and skills *to serve* is the essence of what we do and what clients expect.

Client service is much more than merely a desire to be helpful. It involves transforming that motivation into action by focusing on what is in the client's best interests and then both establishing and accomplishing a course of action necessary to satisfy those interests. Each element of this process is important. Determining what is in the client's best interests requires going beyond a thorough inquiry to determine what the client is trying to accomplish and requires putting yourself in the shoes of the client but with the benefit of your own training and expertise. In other words, successful attorneys know their clients' needs and desires as well as their clients do and are alert to issues their clients have not anticipated. They can then assist their clients in developing strategies that fully accomplish their clients' objectives.

It is important to note that, in carrying out the "game plan," two aspects of client service are critical. First, the entire process must include frequent communication with the client. Too many lawyers, especially those fresh out of law school, focus almost exclusively on the end product – the memorandum, closing papers, or jury verdict – and regard the client as irrelevant, if not a distraction. Almost every client wants to be part of the process, and the lawyer ignores him at the lawyer's peril. From the client's perspective, it is usually impossible to distinguish one legal product from another, but it is quite easy to determine which attorney seemed most interested in being certain the client's needs were being met.

Second, the successful attorney attempts to exceed client expectations whenever possible. For example, he determines at the outset the length of time required to accomplish an action or series of actions and so advises the client (assuming the client's needs do not require a more prompt response). He then delivers the services or product *before* the expected date. Frequent communication with the client and consistently exceeding the client's expectations are key characteristics of a lawyer committed to client service.

Mastery of Legal Concepts and Skills

The importance of a mastery of legal concepts and skills to anyone who wishes to be a successful lawyer is so obvious as to require little discussion. All clients expect their attorneys to know the law and to possess those skills necessary to perform the task at hand. The truly successful attorneys, however, are those whose mastery of legal concepts and skills are so complete as to allow them to achieve creative solutions to client problems.

No one can perform at this level upon leaving law school. Excellent law schools equip their students with fundamental legal concepts and a way of approaching legal issues that provide a foundation for a successful legal career. That educational framework must be followed by years of experience in applying the legal concepts to a variety of factual situations and the testing of various approaches. This experience must in turn be supplemented by continuous efforts at professional development to acquire additional knowledge and improve skills. The process is never complete. Successful lawyers first master basic legal concepts, then the specific laws and skills applicable to their areas of practice, and finally focus on being on the cutting edge of their specialties. There are no shortcuts.

Understanding of Human Nature

Often overlooked in a list of the key characteristics of successful lawyers is an understanding of human nature. A lawyer who has mastered legal concepts and skills incident to his specialty but lacks this characteristic is simply a technician. Even if he is committed to client service, his chances of becoming successful are significantly limited.

Legal issues and problems do not exist in a vacuum. They arise out of relationships between human beings. Ultimate resolution of any dispute or completion of a transaction requires decisions by human beings, whether the resolution is by agreement or a legal proceeding. The greater the number of people involved in the development of the ultimate solution to the problem, the more significant are the human variables that must be addressed.

For example, if two businesses are attempting to consummate a transaction, a number of legal issues will necessarily arise. The resolution of each of those issues will affect the personal "agendas" of both those making the decision and those advising the decision-makers. It is unrealistic to think that all of these parties will take a clinical approach to the transaction and ignore their personal interests. Perhaps some will, but many will not. If the goal is to resolve outstanding issues, as opposed to merely identifying the legal considerations, the attorney must recognize the possible personal agendas and attempt to accommodate them, or at least address them, in some way consistent with whatever options the law allows. The successful lawyer recognizes from the outset both the legal and the human issues at work and takes both into account in developing recommendations.

The importance of understanding human nature is even more obvious in the litigation context. From the moment a lawsuit is even contemplated, the successful trial lawyer is balancing a long list of such considerations. He must predict likely reactions to every conceivable strategy by the judge, jury, witnesses, opposing counsel, co-counsel, client, and, in high-profile matters, the press and the public. He must anticipate, as well, the potential responses of each of these individuals to the strategy of the opposing counsel and to the actions of anyone else involved in the proceeding. The process is dynamic and becomes the true focus of the successful trial lawyer. For some, this process is almost intuitive, but for many it is the result of years of careful observation of people in action.

The best way for any lawyer to approach the human factor in a litigation context is to begin work on any new case by focusing on the end of the case and answering a series of questions: What are my client's goals in this litigation? Who will be the decision-maker – trial judge, jury, appellate court, or opposing counsel (whom I hope to persuade to either throw in the towel or settle)? What will be the most persuasive arguments I can make to that party (or, in many cases, to those parties)? As I try to develop those arguments, what evidentiary or human resistance am I likely to encounter, and from whom? What strategies may I employ to overcome this resistance?

Then, he must step into his opponent's shoes and ask the same series of questions from that viewpoint. Only then can he prepare a strategy that allows him to make his most effective arguments for the decision-makers and prevent his opponent from advancing the opponent's most effective arguments. At all times he must remember that an argument is effective only if the decision-maker finds it to be so.

Every successful trial lawyer follows some form of this process in a disciplined manner. There is no substitute. The human elements of litigation are not just important – they are critical, and the successful trial lawyer knows it.

An important aspect of human nature that frequently comes into play is the difficulty of reaching rational decisions when emotions are high. Simply stated, a successful lawyer knows that neither he nor his client should make important decisions in a case or during the course of a transaction if either is especially angry, elated, disappointed, impatient, or frustrated as a result of a recent event. Almost invariably, the inclination is to be unduly generous or demanding, neither of which is likely to produce a favorable outcome for the client. Every transaction or trial yields one or more moments when emotions do not control the decision-making process, and it is then that the resolution of issues should be attempted. Likewise, the successful attorney is alert to the emotional reactions of his opponent that might produce opportunities for a favorable outcome and seizes those opportunities.

Of course, these are just examples of how the human element affects an attorney's efforts to serve his client. The overriding point is that the successful attorney not only recognizes the importance of this factor, but he also consistently uses it to his advantage.

Communication Skills

All of the foregoing considerations achieve maximum impact when the lawyer is an effective communicator. Unquestionably, all lawyers can communicate to some extent, and most do so far better than the average person. Somewhat surprisingly, however, many attorneys have never really mastered the art of communicating effectively in a variety of contexts. In recent years, attorneys in a number of large firms have commented on writing deficiencies they observe in new associates. The concern is not that these new lawyers struggle to write complete sentences. Rather, it is that many do not organize the material in a clear, logical way and take the reader through the material with appropriate transitions. Furthermore, they observe that the language used is not simple and direct. Any attorney taken to task over his writing style should take the criticism seriously and seek help immediately. A number of legal writing programs have surfaced in recent years, perhaps because of these concerns. An attorney must be able to write clearly and concisely if he is to be successful.

Of equal importance are oral presentation skills. Attorneys who are excellent public speakers have a significant advantage in almost every area of practice. Even those who are not called upon to address judges or juries find themselves sooner or later making presentations to boards of directors, business groups, or their peers. The quality of these presentations will influence those who are in a position to determine whether the attorneys will ultimately be successful. In addition, the presentation itself is almost always designed either to inform or to persuade the group to whom it is given; that is, it has a purpose. The purpose is rarely accomplished if the presentation is not effective; hence, an opportunity to succeed is squandered. The attorney who has not developed skills in this area should seek courses in public speaking, especially those that afford videotaping as an option.

One other aspect of communication is important for the attorney who wishes to be successful: the ability to lead meetings. Attorneys frequently find themselves in legal, business, or community meetings, and almost as frequently are eventually afforded the opportunity to lead the group. Leading meetings effectively is an art form in itself, and few people do it effectively. Those who do assume greater and greater leadership roles in contexts that enhance their abilities to be successful. A short course on leading meetings is well worth the effort.

Again, communication is where the commitment to client service, mastery of legal concepts and skills, and an understanding of human nature come together to present attorneys opportunities for success. They can seize those opportunities if they communicate effectively.

Professionalism

A successful attorney adheres to the standards and ideals of his profession. At a minimum, this involves practicing within the bounds of the law and the canons of ethics in his state. But it really means much more. To be truly successful, an attorney must gain and maintain the respect of his peers. He knows that to do so he must not only demonstrate his overall competence or even an extraordinary level of skill, but must also establish consistently that he can be trusted in all of his dealings with other attorneys and the public at large. Breach of that trust usually stains a legal career forever. To state the obvious, an attorney who proves not to be trustworthy is not trusted. Integrity is therefore the most important characteristic of a successful attorney. Without it, his individual "successes" have no meaning, and his purported commitment to client service is more properly viewed as a commitment to winning.

Integrity is simply a personal commitment to act honestly and honorably at all times, to be true to oneself, to do what is right, regardless of the consequences. In many ways it is an internal compass that automatically steers us in the proper direction without the intervention of outside forces. Acting with integrity is its own reward, but it also enhances the attorney's ability to be successful in any transaction or proceeding. A lawyer whose integrity is beyond question can obviously be trusted with far more significant matters than one whose integrity is in doubt. A successful lawyer's word is his bond, and he is treated accordingly.

Professionalism also includes the manner in which lawyers deal with each other. Successful lawyers treat their peers and others with respect. They do not need to belittle other people or humiliate them to be successful. They do not distinguish between their peers on the basis of race, religion, or gender. Their talent, skills, and commitment to client service are sufficient in themselves, and anyone they deal with knows it.

Simply put, truly successful lawyers represent the ideals of their profession. Those characteristics are both the foundation for and the reflection of their success.

Ability to Juggle

One of the greatest challenges a lawyer faces is allocating his time appropriately among a variety of different interests, each of which has a legitimate demand on his time. The old saying is, "The law is a jealous mistress." It means the practice of law can be an all-consuming task, leaving little time for other activities. To have a successful legal career, an attorney must find ways to achieve an overall balance in his practice and between his practice and life on the outside.

If one is committed to client service, this commitment alone can be a full-time job. As indicated earlier, each client deserves considerable attention, and a commitment to providing that level of attention to the client is a prerequisite to success. Realistically, to survive financially, most lawyers must serve a number of clients simultaneously. The result is competing demands for the lawyer's time and a need to juggle these demands effectively. A senior lawyer once said that almost any young attorney who did reasonably well in law school and has a minimum level of experience can handle a single matter well if he has all the time he needs to spend on it. The art of the successful attorney is being able to represent simultaneously a number of clients on a variety of matters and do so effectively. The lawyer must develop proficiency in a number of areas to accomplish this task.

First, he must master the various skill sets I've already mentioned. His ability to juggle various matters simultaneously will be hindered by ineffectiveness in any of these areas simply because it takes longer to perform those tasks that one has not yet mastered. Failure to take the time necessary for each task is not an answer because the result will be negatively affected. In other words, one must take the time early in one's career to develop all of the necessary skills, so he can go faster later.

Second, the attorney must develop a satisfactory time management system. Various programs, books, and articles offer suggestions, and the key is finding what works best for the individual attorney. The most important points, however, are that there must be a system, and it must include a process for setting priorities among the competing demands.

Third, the attorney must control the demands on his time instead of letting the demands control him. The latter leads to frustration and occasionally depression or more serious consequences. Part of the solution is recognizing when the demands are overwhelming and help is needed. Under no circumstances should the attorney mislead the client or opposing counsel or the court about when a task will be completed or make promises he cannot likely keep. Such actions can lead to disastrous short-term consequences and, on a long-term basis, make the attorney less trustworthy.

Finally, the tired and overworked attorney cannot ignore communicating with the client on the basis that he is working so hard on the client's business. Remember that it is the client's problem, that the client wants to be involved, and that the goal is client satisfaction with the services. This means returning all phone calls, discussing frankly with the client the status of all matters, and being candid about competing demands on one's time. Most clients understand that lawyers have other clients and do not want to be responsible for paying for all of an attorney's hours every day.

In many ways a greater challenge is presented by the desire to balance career and family obligations. Each can make a strong claim for all of the attorney's time. At the same time, there is no direct confrontation between career and family. Both focus their demands on the attorney and look to him to resolve the competing claims. He must constantly remind himself that he alone controls his schedule, and he alone is in a position to make each party aware of his need to spend certain time with the other.

For example, the attorney should start by sharing with his family what he is trying to accomplish in his career. He should stress that practicing law is serving other people and that his doing so is valuable to society as well as his clients.

He must make them see the value in what he is doing and share in his desire to serve others. At the same time, the attorney must demonstrate to his family by his actions that ultimately they come first. He should affirmatively seek out opportunities to be with his family and attend important events in the lives of his children. It is always easy to push aside a family event and fill it with a client activity under the theory that it is good for business or the client or even the family because of the potential financial rewards. Most clients, however, face similar conflicts and can both understand and respect their lawyer's desire to spend time with family. Frankly, if the client is unreasonably demanding in this regard, the attorney should avoid a long-term relationship with this client. Again, this balance is not easy to achieve, but it is difficult to consider an attorney successful if his personal life is in tatters because of his pursuit of his career.

Service to Others

People who go to law school are blessed with certain talents and skills that can be used to advance the interests of the community and the legal profession. A successful attorney finds time during the course of his career to serve both groups. The service can be through community or bar associations, one-on-one with people in need, or even through the political process. The opportunities for service are many, and the attorney can select the ones that appeal most to him.

Knowing the demands already facing a lawyer, one may wonder how any attorney can find time for these activities, but the reality is that many do. In fact, if a survey were taken of members as to which senior lawyers in their communities they considered most successful, those who balanced career, family, and community service would win every time. Isn't that the ultimate definition of success?

Recognizing, nonetheless, the difficulties inherent in balancing all of these activities, one suggestion might be helpful. Remember that a career spans several decades. Family demands are greater during some of those years than in others. Likewise, one's practice may consume a greater part of one's day in some years than in others. As long as service to the community and profession remain a priority, they will find their appropriate places in one's schedule during the course of a career.

Have we addressed all of the key characteristics of a successful lawyer? Consider them in combination and then decide by asking these questions:

1. Can anyone seriously argue that an attorney is not successful if he is committed to client service, has mastered legal concepts and skills, understands human nature, communicates effectively, conducts himself in a professional manner, effectively balances competing client and family demands, and serves his community and profession?
2. Can anyone seriously argue that an attorney is truly successful if he lacks any of these characteristics?

The answer to each is obvious. One final question might also be asked: Would the answer to either of these questions change if the attorney were financially successful? Of course not. Techniques for increasing the profitability of a legal practice are valuable from the standpoint of improving a lawyer's financial status. They do not, however, define a successful legal career.

Success in a Law Firm

As the discussion thus far demonstrates and generations of successful attorneys have proved, one need not be a member of a law firm to become a successful lawyer. Most young attorneys, however, do join firms, and many find their way to either a mid-size or a large firm. Frequently, the decision is made on the basis that doing so has become the accepted way to begin a legal career or because of the size of the salaries being offered or in response to the fear of trying to launch a career without any practical experience. A more careful, disciplined approach to choosing a law firm and identifying one's future role in that firm would increase the likelihood of success for both the individual and the firm.

Law firms provide numerous advantages for their attorneys who are intent on a successful career. Typically, they afford the lawyer greater access to sophisticated legal work than he could attract on his own. They also put at his disposal substantial resources that are helpful in providing the necessary work. These resources include technology, a library, work product from other similar matters, a reputation and status in the legal community, additional attorneys to share the load, and frequently professional development opportunities. That is, except for the intangible qualities associated with a successful legal career, the firm can provide or at least assist the attorney in acquiring the necessary characteristics. The young lawyer should ascertain at the outset that the firm in question can provide these advantages. If it cannot, he should look elsewhere.

Of equal importance is the need to examine the more intangible qualities of the firm. Specifically, the prospective recruit should ascertain the firm's core values and determine whether they are consistent with his own. Do they include, for instance, such important qualities as integrity, commitment to client service, respect for other members of the firm and other attorneys outside the firm, and a desire to serve the community and the profession? If these core values are not present, and especially if the culture of the firm runs counter to one or more of these values, the attorney should recognize the limitations that practicing with this particular firm will place on his attempts to secure a successful career. If they are present, the path to success has been laid, and association with the firm will maximize his chances to become successful.

The ideal firm will also feature strong leadership, a clear vision, a sense of teamwork, and communication. These characteristics ensure that the firm will continue to provide the necessary resources for professional growth and, in turn, a successful career.

It is extremely important that the attorney recognize his own responsibilities in functioning within the law firm while he pursues a successful career. These obligations include the following:

1. Although many of his early assignments will require only that he perform specific legal research, and a salary bonus program may encourage his spending substantial time on these activities, the attorney must devote a significant amount of his time to acquiring the various skills that are characteristic of successful attorneys. He cannot afford to sacrifice the long term for the short term.

2. The attorney must discipline himself to handle each task he is assigned as well as he possibly can and demonstrate to everyone involved that he will handle all matters with integrity and professionalism. In so doing, he will not only lay the foundation for a solid future

with firm, but also develop the self-discipline necessary for a successful legal career.

3. Human nature is as strong a factor in the operation of a law firm and teams within a law firm as it is in the client matters the attorney will handle. The attorney should be alert for all personal agendas of those with whom he is working, develop plans for dealing with them effectively, and consider the effort required to be time well spent because of the skills he acquires.

4. As a member of the firm, the attorney should work hard to assist the firm in its efforts to accomplish its mission and preserve its core values. For the foreseeable future, the success of the firm and the attorney's own success are inextricably linked. He helps himself by advancing the interests of the firm.

5. The attorney must assist the firm in performing those tasks incident to its being a profitable business without allowing the firm's financial success to define him or his career.

6. The attorney can usually control the pace of his progress in the firm. He does not have to achieve partnership by a certain date unless he imposes that date on himself. He alone is therefore responsible for the time spent on client business, as compared to that which

is devoted to family or community and professional service. Obviously, he must perform effectively at certain levels of billable work to maintain a relationship with the firm, but he is otherwise free to chart his own course and pursue a successful career.

7. The attorney should identify from among the partnership ranks those attorneys who appear most successful (as measured by the extent to which they possess the characteristics identified above) and seek opportunities to learn from them.

An attorney who examines carefully a prospective firm to be sure it will maximize his chances for success and who assumes his own responsibilities in the relationship will take a giant step along the road to the career he seeks.

The Ultimate Responsibility

The practice of law has changed considerably during the past 25 years and will likely experience even more significant changes in the next 25. Continued technological improvements, the shrinking business world, accounting firms' assumption of a greater portion of the legal market, and the increasing number of law firm mergers suggest that some of the changes are likely to be significant.

What is constant, however, are the characteristics of a successful legal career and what a lawyer must do to achieve that goal. Commitment to client service, professionalism, and community and professional service will continue to be the intangible qualities that form the foundation for success. Mastery of legal concepts and skills, an understanding of human nature, development of strong communication skills, and the ability to juggle competing demands on one's time will remain the necessary tools. Law firms whose core values and mission are consistent with the intangible qualities and that provide access to the tools necessary for success will attract those driven to succeed and afford a fertile ground for their development. Ultimately, however, success will depend then, as now, on the individual – his goals, his skills, and his dedication to a life of professional growth and excellence.

Keith W. Vaughan, chair of the Firm Management Committee of Womble Carlyle Sandridge & Rice, PLLC, has extensive experience in litigation matters involving business, products liability, toxic tort, and environmental issues. For several years, he has served as national coordinating counsel for a Fortune 500 company in products liability litigation. During his 20-plus year career, he has tried numerous jury and bench trials, handled various administrative proceedings, and argued a wide range of matters in appellate courts.

Mr. Vaughan is a member of the American and North Carolina Bar Associations and a member of the American Inns of Court. He received his BA, cum laude, from Wake Forest University and his JD, cum laude, from the University of Georgia, where he was editor-in-chief of the Georgia Law Review.

SKILLS FOR SUCCESSFUL LAWYERING

KEITH C. WETMORE

Morrison & Foerster LLP

Chair

Style, Culture, and Moral Code

The art of lawyering lies in combining technical skills, which are scientific in nature, with intuition about both your client's needs and the anticipated behavior of other parties. In a business transaction, you provide to your client not only what the client has said they want, but also a good instinct as to what the client would want under other circumstances that may arise. Additionally, you make a guess as to where the other parties might seek to exploit your client in the future, and provide advance protection against those efforts. In litigation, the job is quite similar: You must know where your party wants to go, and you must also know the opposing parties and where they will go with each move you make. Therein lies the art of lawyering, I believe.

Certain skills are essential for lawyer-client relations. First is intellect. Second are listening skills, a service bias, and commitment. You do not represent the law; you represent a client who has real needs. It is your job to pursue those needs even if you might disagree with the client as to how to achieve them. You should discuss with the client whether there are other needs that might be equally as important. The most frequent disappointment in recruiting lawyers out of law school is with people who miss the point that a client is looking for someone to represent them, warts and all. They need to be listened to and tended to.

I am a big believer that every lawyer needs to find her or his own voice. You do not become a fine lawyer by sitting beside and mimicking one senior lawyer. That is not your voice, and it will not be convincing. I believe it is very important – especially when looking at the success of women and lawyers of color – that young lawyers who are not just like everybody else in the firm have multiple role models to help them find that voice. You need to triangulate between culturally accurate examples for your voice and your experience so that you can speak with authority. You should not sound like someone putting on the costume of a Wall Street lawyer if that style does not work for you. This is not to say that there isn't some conformity in narrowing the range; you do not see people screaming and throwing books at each other or otherwise behaving outside the zone of business behavior in the midst of sophisticated transactions. Certainly, there are very different techniques as to how people get their point across, and you need to use a technique that works for you.

Turning to my own voice – as reflected in my practice – I am not very good at subterfuge. Generally I lay cards on the table. Big surprises and "gotchas" after the deal closes are not my style; they undercut moral stature in a negotiation. I am not sure the strategy I described would work very effectively for a litigator. I am accustomed to transactions where people are business partners and will have to live with each other under a legal regime that the lawyers craft. Going into it in an honest, straightforward manner has always worked best for me.

In that vein, I would note that the entire mechanic of high-level business transactions depends upon a certain code of conduct in connection with the transactions. A team of lawyers will stay up all night getting the final documents ready and laying them all out in neat piles with dozens of signature pages to be signed by each side, including the parties who are not their clients. On the morning of the closing, the opponents show up, sign the signature pages, and leave them there on the table. They trust that the lawyers will attach them to the documents that were negotiated, and that they did not spend the night pulling together completely different documents, or that they did not substitute pages. In a truly adversarial system, you might say it's every woman for herself; if you were not smart enough to read every page before you signed it, then you get what you deserve. If we did that, we would never get the deals closed.

Instead, there exists an ethical code of how to go about doing these things. We don't do things behind each other's back in either a legal sense or a documentation sense. Similarly, we fax signature pages around all the time, and everybody trusts everybody else to attach them to the right document. We send executed signature pages days ahead of closing sometimes, and we hold onto them until we are done. One slip from that standard completely undermines the credibility of the individual and the firm involved. It is part of the culture of transactional lawyering; you hardly ever see breaches of that code. In litigation, the engine lies in being able to rely on each other's words with respect to extensions and various procedural things that need to be worked out. Litigators regularly accommodate each other in ways that allow the litigation to go forward.

Keeping Current

In addition to being a convincing negotiator and an ethical facilitator, transactional lawyers are expected to bring broad-based perspective to the engagement. Part of what one does in building a practice is getting into a deal flow that allows you to know what parties to a transaction are expecting in a certain context. A lawyer gets there only by being in the deal flow. My clients look to me to have a broader perspective than their own. They assume that at 45, I have seen more syndicated credit agreements than they have. I have three or four rolling at any given time, and they are working on one or two. The clients expect us to be links between themselves and market practice.

Finally, of course, a lawyer needs to balance personal and professional commitments. My parents were in the service business. I don't remember my father taking a vacation longer than a couple of hours, and when he was away, he was always checking the phone. To some extent, my life is a lot more manageable than his life ever was. Because law is a service profession, people require personal attention. It is necessary to have a high degree of individual lawyer commitment to see that clients feel attended to, but that doesn't prohibit negotiating with clients about your own unavailability. For the most part, I find clients to be very forgiving, and my partners are also very understanding.

Challenges of Leadership

It should come as no surprise that the most significant challenge to lawyers in leadership positions is putting ego on the shelf. There is a lot of press today about the decentralized corporation. There is an effort to decentralize thinking so you can let a thousand flowers bloom in terms of corporate strategy. In many respects, the American law firm is a fabulous laboratory for independent thinking, and the nurturing of independence in organizational management. I do not have the skill set that would allow me to direct R&D strategy for a half-billion-dollar-a-year organization. Fortunately, I don't have to do this because I have 300 partners, most of whom spend a great deal of time thinking about our institutional R&D. We use the organizational structure to nurture some of their ideas and to stifle others; however, people feel a very personal investment in a professional organization in their practice, and they are empowered to innovate.

The hardest part is balancing the extent to which an organization needs a leader with the extent to which a professional organization needs to function by consultation and independence. The real engines are the business generators. My highest priorities lie in nurturing the racehorses; the people who are key to important practices need to feel supported, and the organization needs them to continue to be productive through the course of a long and demanding career. I balance the consultative function concerning those who appropriately believe they have a voice in the process with the need, in some cases, to get the entire firm marching in the same direction, if not in lockstep.

While managing a firm in turbulent markets, I work with a couple of basic tenets: Nothing lasts forever, and things will be different eventually. The trick is doing what you need to do in the short term without losing sight of what you will need when things turn around. To some extent it requires institutional patience. Every firm could find a way to make itself as busy as it was before the market turbulence if they cut deeply enough. The questions are: What do you do when you have a turnaround? Who do you do it with? What market opportunities did you miss while other people were busy hacking and slashing? What did you fail to exploit? I also try to sell the message that you have to expect some slow areas, or you won't be properly staffed for the busy times or the turnaround.

Establishing a fair compensation system is critical. People are very perceptive; a number of subtle signals indicate what works and does not work in terms of management. The compensation system of a law firm is arguably its DNA. If you reward certain behavior, you can count on having more of it. You need to be constantly thinking of the compensation system: Am I rewarding behaviors I want to see practiced more broadly, and am I choosing not to reward behaviors I don't want to see? If you look at compensation, it will tell you a great deal about some law firms and about what behavior you are likely to see there.

The Lawyer's Role in Society

The law is arguably several professions. What I do as a transactional lawyer is different from the work of my mother's estate lawyer or the work of the lawyer who helped her buy her house. We collectively play a different role in society.

My practice – and the practice of transactional lawyers – is like investment banking without the capital requirement; it is part of the grease of the economic engine, and it is impossible to generate GDP without us, for better or worse. We are a constructive facilitator and risk manager. People feel confident investing in the U.S. because they have confidence in a system of justice that allows disputes to be resolved in a rational way. It might be excruciatingly expensive, but the outcomes fall within anticipated ranges based on the conduct involved.

We worry that the U.S. justice system will get a black eye for not being a predictable means of solving disputes. In a very important other aspect, which addresses the real needs of human beings every day, lawyers are the gatekeepers to justice. Having been given a monopoly in that regard, accordingly, we owe a duty to the body politic to give back to the community, to perform *pro bono* services, and to participate in the development of the law. Too often those of us who operate at the large transaction level forget that we also have a duty to the profession and to the community, and we had better deliver on it if we expect the government to allow us to continue to stand between individuals and the justice system.

The Past and Future of Legal Issues

In the technology boom of the late 1990s, we saw a transformation in the role of lawyering in the sense of the lawyer becoming the deal-maker; a lawyer was as valuable for her Rolodex as for her skill set. In contemplating whether this is a permanent change, I lean toward the conclusion that in the smaller-company representation sector, the role of lawyering has forever been changed. Fortune 500 companies don't need that skill set, but entrepreneurs do; it has now become an article of faith that an entrepreneur will not obtain a lawyer who cannot help on that front. That is one of the significant changes in the style of practice rather than in the law itself.

In the present day, we witness the increased criminalization of corporate misconduct, and we also see some erosion of the concept of the corporate shield against liability. These are not entirely the wrong things for the legal system to be focusing on, but it will be a time of turmoil in boardrooms and CFO offices as we come to grips with what the post-Enron and post-WorldCom world looks like in U.S. security laws and U.S. corporate governance.

Regarding the state of lawyers today, my purely personal view is that class action is the source of many of the bad things that people think about lawyers. There are also stories about people who could find no one to represent them except in that context, but the instances of enormous settlements where individuals seem lost in the shuffle trouble me very much. Individuals receive little out of the litigation, as most is consumed by legal fees. It is dealt with as a cost of business in corporate America to pay off the trial lawyers. But there is some evidence of reform. Our former partner, Judge Bill Alsup from the U.S. District Court for the Northern District of California, has done some innovative work on making law firms bid to encourage efficiencies in pursuing clients.

Keith C. Wetmore is the chair of Morrison & Foerster LLP, a leading international law firm with approximately 1,000 lawyers in 18 offices around the world. As chair of the firm,

Mr. Wetmore takes the lead in setting policy and providing strategic direction to the firm, while overseeing the operation of a partnership with approximately a half-billion dollars in annual revenues.

Before becoming chair, Mr. Wetmore was managing partner of the firm's San Francisco office. He also led the firm's 50-lawyer Finance and Infrastructure practice, bringing to his engagements 20 years' experience in debt and lease finance, both domestic and international.

Mr. Wetmore continues to represent money center banks as agent in syndicated credit facilities, including multi-billion dollar working capital and acquisition financings, as well as smaller transactions, with particular emphasis in the technology and forest products sectors.

Mr. Wetmore received his BA in economics from Northwestern University. He graduated, magna cum laude, from the University of Michigan Law School, where he served as articles editor for the Michigan Law Review and was elected to the Order of the Coif. He then clerked for Judge J. Edward Lumbard on the U.S. Court of Appeals for the Second Circuit. He associated with Morrison &

Foerster in 1982 and became a partner of the firm in 1986. Mr. Wetmore is currently a member of the Board of Directors of the San Francisco AIDS Foundation.

BUSINESS INTELLIGENCE PUBLICATIONS & SERVICES

THE C-LEVEL LIBRARY™

The C-Level Library enables you and your team to quickly get up to speed on a topic, understand the issues that drive an industry, identify new business opportunities, and profit from the knowledge of the world's leading executives. Thousands of books, briefs, reports and essays are broken down and organized by Aspatore Business Editors in a user-friendly format to ensure easy maneuvering and efficient researching. In just 10 minutes, you can be up to speed on any topic, or lay the groundwork to thoroughly research any industry or job position in The C-Level Library. Aspatore annually publishes C-Level executives from over half the Global 500, the top 250 professional services firms, the fastest-growing 250 private companies, MP/Chairs from over half the 250 largest law firms and leading executives representing nearly every industry. Content is updated weekly and available for use in various formats - as-is online, printed, copied and pasted into a PDA, and even emailed directly to you. Speak intelligently with anyone, in any industry, on any topic. Subscribe to The C-Level Library.

LICENSE/BULK ORDERS OF CONTENT PUBLISHED BY ASPATORE

For information on bulk purchases or licensing content published by Aspatore for a web site, corporate intranet, extranet, newsletter, direct mail, book or in another format, please email store@aspatore.com. For orders over 100 books or chapter excerpts, company logos and additional text can be added to the book.

CORPORATE PUBLISHING GROUP (AN ASPATORE OWNED COMPANY)

Corporate Publishing Group (CPG) provides companies with on-demand writing and editing resources from the world's best writing teams. Our clients come to CPG for the writing and editing of books, reports, speeches, company brochures, press releases, product literature, web site copy and other publications. This enables companies to save time and money, reduce headcount, and ensure polished and articulate written pieces. Each client is assigned a CPG team devoted to their company, which works on their projects throughout the course of a year on an as-needed basis and helps generate new written documents, review and edit documents already written, and provide an outside perspective before a document "goes public" in order to help companies maintain a polished image both internally and externally. Clients have included companies in all industries and disciplines, ranging from financial to technology to law firms, and are represented by over half of the Fortune 500. For more information please e-mail rpollock@corporateapublishinggroup.com or visit www.CorporatePublishingGroup.com.

SMARTPACKS ™ — GET UP TO SPEED FAST!

SmartPacks help you determine what to read so that you can get up to speed on a new topic fast, with the right books, magazines, web sites, and other publications (from every major publisher in the world including over 30,000 sources). The 2-step process involves an approximately 15 minute phone call and then a report written by Aspatore Business Editors and mailed (or emailed) to you the following day (rush options available).

ASPATORE C-LEVEL RESEARCH™

Aspatore Business Editors are available to help individuals, companies, and professionals in any industry perform research on a given topic on either a one-time or a consistent monthly basis. Aspatore Business Editors, with their deep industry expertise at getting access to the right information across every medium, can serve as an external librarian/researcher for all your research needs.

ESTABLISH YOUR OWN BUSINESS LIBRARY™

Work with Aspatore editors to identify 50-5,000 individual books from all publishers, and purchase them at special rates for a corporate or personal library.

To Order or For Customized Suggestions From an Aspatore Business Editor, Please Call 1-866-Aspatore (277-2867) Or Visit www.Aspatore.com

Best Selling Books

(Also Available Individually At Your Local Bookstore)

REFERENCE

Business Travel Bible (BTB) – Must Have Information for Business Travelers

Business Grammar, Style & Usage – Rules for Articulate and Polished Business Writing and Speaking

ExecRecs – Executive Recommendations For The Best Products, Services & Intelligence Executives Use to Excel

The C-Level Test – Business IQ & Personality Test for Professionals of All Levels

The Business Translator-Business Words, Phrases & Customs in Over 90 Languages

MANAGEMENT/CONSULTING

Leading CEOs – CEOs Reveal the Secrets to Leadership & Profiting in Any Economy

Leading Consultants – Industry Leaders Share Their Knowledge on the Art of Consulting

Recession Profiteers – How to Profit in a Recession & Wipe Out the Competition

Managing & Profiting in a Down Economy – Leading CEOs Reveal the Secrets to Increased Profits and Success in a Turbulent Economy

Leading Women – What It Takes to Succeed & Have It All in the 21st Century

Become a CEO – The Golden Rules to Rising the Ranks of Leadership

Leading Deal Makers – Leveraging Your Position and the Art of Deal Making

The Art of Deal Making – The Secrets to the Deal Making Process

Empower Profits – The Secrets to Cutting Costs & Making Money in ANY Economy

Building an Empire – The 10 Most Important Concepts to Focus a Business on the Way to Dominating the Business World

Management Brainstormers – Question Blocks & Idea Worksheets

TECHNOLOGY

Leading CTOs – The Secrets to the Art, Science & Future of Technology

Software Product Management – Managing Software Development from Idea to Development to Marketing to Sales

The Telecommunications Industry – Leading CEOs Share Their Knowledge on The Future of the Telecommunications Industry

Know What the CTO Knows – The Tricks of the Trade and Ways for Anyone to Understand the Language of the Techies

Web 2.0 AC (After Crash) – The Resurgence of the Internet and Technology Economy

The Semiconductor Industry – Leading CEOs Share Their Knowledge on the Future of Semiconductors

Techie Talk – The Tricks of the Trade and Ways to Develop, Implement and Capitalize on the Best Technologies in the World

Technology Brainstormers – Question Blocks & Idea Development Worksheets

VENTURE CAPITAL/ENTREPRENEURIAL

Term Sheets & Valuations – A Detailed Look at the Intricacies of Term Sheets & Valuations

Deal Terms – The Finer Points of Deal Structures, Valuations, Term Sheets, Stock Options and Getting Deals Done

Leading Deal Makers – Leveraging Your Position and the Art of Deal Making

The Art of Deal Making – The Secrets to the Deal Making Process

Hunting Venture Capital – Understanding the VC Process and Capturing an Investment

The Golden Rules of Venture Capitalists – Valuing Companies, Identifying Opportunities, Detecting Trends, Term Sheets and Valuations

To Order or For Customized Suggestions From an Aspatore Business Editor, Please Call 1-866-Aspatore (277-2867) Or Visit www.Aspatore.com

Entrepreneurial Momentum – Gaining Traction for Businesses of All Sizes to Take the Step to the Next Level

The Entrepreneurial Problem Solver – Entrepreneurial Strategies for Identifying Opportunities in the Marketplace

Entrepreneurial Brainstormers – Question Blocks & Idea Development Worksheets

LEGAL

Privacy Matters – Leading Privacy Visionaries Share Their Knowledge on How Privacy on the Internet Will Affect Everyone

Leading Lawyers – Leading Managing Partners Reveal the Secrets to Professional and Personal Success as a Lawyer

The Innovative Lawyer – Leading Lawyers Share Their Knowledge on Using Innovation to Gain an Edge

Leading Labor Lawyers – Labor Chairs Reveal the Secrets to the Art & Science of Labor Law

Leading Litigators – Litigation Chairs Revel the Secrets to the Art & Science of Litigation

Leading IP Lawyers – IP Chairs Reveal the Secrets to the Art & Science of IP Law

Leading Patent Lawyers – The & Science of Patent Law

Leading Deal Makers – Leveraging Your Position and the Art of Deal Making

Legal Brainstormers – Question Blocks & Idea Development Worksheets

FINANCIAL

Textbook Finance – The Fundamentals We Should All Know (And Remember) About Finance

Know What the CFO Knows – Leading CFOs Reveal What the Rest of Us Should Know About the Financial Side of Companies

Leading Accountants – The Golden Rules of Accounting & the Future of the Accounting Industry and Profession

Leading Investment Bankers – Leading I-Bankers Reveal the Secrets to the Art & Science of Investment Banking

The Financial Services Industry – The Future of the Financial Services Industry & Professions

Empower Profits – The Secrets to Cutting Costs & Making Money in ANY Economy

MARKETING/ADVERTISING/PR

Leading Marketers – Leading Chief Marketing Officers Reveal the Secrets to Building a Billion Dollar Brand

Emphatic Marketing – Getting the World to Notice and Use Your Company

Leading Advertisers – Advertising CEOs Reveal the Tricks of the Advertising Profession

The Art of PR – Leading PR CEOs Reveal the Secrets to the Public Relations Profession

The Golden Rules of Marketing – Leading Marketers Reveal the Secrets to Marketing, Advertising and Building Successful Brands

PR Visionaries – PR CEOS Reveal the Golden Rules of PR

Textbook Marketing – The Fundamentals We Should All Know (And Remember) About Marketing

Know What the VP of Marketing Knows – What Everyone Should Know About Marketing, For the Rest of Us Not in Marketing

Marketing Brainstormers – Question Blocks & Idea Development Worksheets

Guerrilla Marketing – The Best of Guerrilla Marketing-Big Marketing Ideas For a Small Budget

The Art of Sales – The Secrets for Anyone to Become a Rainmaker and Why Everyone in a Company Should be a Salesperson

Inside the Minds:
Leading Lawyers
The Art & Science of Being a Successful Lawyer

Acknowledgements and Dedications

William H. Brewster

This chapter is dedicated to my wife, Karen, and our children, Kristina, Will, and Katie.

Keith C. Wetmore

The author thanks his colleague Karl Christiansen for his editorial assistance.

ASPATORE

C-Level Business Intelligence™